FOCUS OR FAILURE:
AMERICA AT THE CROSSROADS
WHERE ARE YOU?

pg 25-26 ". ATTITUDE IS DETERMINED BY
ACTION ? HABITS ARE
OUR ATTITUDES IN ACTION.

First Edition 1998
EXECUTIVE BOOKS
Life Management Services, Inc.
206 W. Allen Street
Mechanicsburg, PA 17055
800-233-2665

Printed in the United States of America

ISBN 0-937539-31-7
ISBN 0-937539-35-X (PAPERBACK EDITION)
LCCN #98-87240

DEDICATION

For my mother and father Jim and Jehri Amos; my wife
Micki; my daughter Holly Amos; my daughter Heather
and son-in-law Michael...my family.

MISSION

To re-awaken America to the heritage we all share.
To cherish excellence and celebrate people who won't give up.
To value moral triumph more than material success.
And, to recognize that even in the worst circumstances we
retain an unassailable freedom to control our attitudes
toward our circumstances.

ACKNOWLEDGMENTS

I have a passion for books. An inveterate reader, I form warm personal relationships with books and, through their work, the authors. Guides, mentors, counselors, and educators books have filled my life and colored my imagination. I cannot take credit for the knowledge these writers have so freely given. If I have inadvertently not ascribed to you a thought, an idea or phrase, I assure you no malice of forethought was intended. Nonetheless, I am grateful for the many ideas and exhortations to think and grow that these wonderful tomes have given me through the years. As Elie Wiesel said, "There is a divine beauty in learning. To learn means to accept the postulate that life did not begin at birth. Others have been here before me and I walk in their footsteps. The books I have read were composed by a generation of fathers and sons, mothers and daughters, teachers and disciples. I am the sum total of their experiences, and so are you."

I am particularly grateful to Judy Erickson and Gia Derrick, my past and present Executive Assistants, and friends, without whose diligence, patience and support this work would not have become a reality.

AUTHOR'S NOTE:

This is not a religious book...anymore than "forgiveness" or "values" or "love" are exclusively religious terms. This is a book about fundamentals and basics. Focal points. There are twelve chapters or fundamentals to master that I believe can help transform the heart of Americans and America. Each fundamental will have within it other recommended reading and reference material as an aid to ongoing mastery. I hope you find this work enjoyable and valuable but I hasten to point out this is not a game, but a way of changing the moral climate and effectiveness of our country. Things do matter. Often life feels like it is a game being played by men and women who excel at gameship. "Our life in this country, the sacrifices that have been made for this country, the lives that have been given to this country, are not a game. My parents' lives were not a game."[1]

And as my friend Charlie "Tremendous" Jones is fond of saying, "You are the message." Power has never made America or American business great. Goodness and virtue have. "All around me is the sound of moral decay. I hear the sound of America crying. And it is no game."[2]

We have been the recipients of the choicest bounties of Heaven. We have been preserved these many years in peace and prosperity. We have grown in numbers, wealth, and power as no other nation has grown. But we have forgotten God. We have forgotten the gracious hand which preserved us in peace, and multiplied and enriched and strengthened us; and we have vainly imagined, in the deceitfulness of our hearts, that all these blessings were produced by some superior wisdom and virtue of our own.

Intoxicated with unbroken success, we have become too self-sufficient to feel the necessity of redeeming and preserving grace, too proud to pray to the God that made us!

It behooves us, then, to humble ourselves before the offended Power to confess our national sins, and to pray for clemency and forgiveness.

-Abraham Lincoln

FOCUS OR FAILURE:
AMERICA AT THE CROSSROADS
WHERE ARE YOU?

BY
JAMES H. AMOS, JR.

TABLE OF CONTENTS

PROLOGUE

There is something monumental happening in the world today. The cacophony of sound bites shroud a persistent, pervasive and irrevocable feeling of uncertainty and despair that seems to be enveloping the globe. The United States, it appears, has buried its mortal enemy. The death of both an idea and an empire, Communism and the Soviet Union, had kept millions of baby boomers vacillating between fear and hate for fifty years. The world paused long enough to observe that the largest number of free countries in history could now be listed statistically and American culture was taking root around the globe. Some people even began to talk of Pax Americana, a new age of American business and peace.

At home, while Americans are enjoying one of the longest and most prolonged economic upswings in recent memory, legitimate victories such as that over Communism seem to offer no joy. At a mundane level, practical solutions to leftover economic problems continue to go wanting and social problems that began with moral questions still appear to have no end and continue to plague bureaucracy. In a rapidly changing world, no one seems to know what role the United States or American business will play. Heading into the millennium America seems to be directionally lacking purpose and meaning. We are at war within ourselves. It is a civil war for the soul of our nation. As Ray Bradbury pointed out in the April 3rd 1998 *Wall Street Journal*, "How come we are one of the greatest nations in the world...and yet there is this feeling of doom? How come, while our president walks wounded, we ourselves jog along nicely...but under a dark cloud that says something awful is about to happen."[3]

People are angry and alienation appears to be the psychological disease of the day. "The future just doesn't seem to be what it used to be. The future most of us grew up with was the one that was supposed to be the past only more so – larger disposable income, speedier interurban travel, higher fidelity, faster food. The futurism of more recent years, dominated by environmental alarms, differs only in its message. The methodology is the same: more people, less food, oil and ozone.

Nowadays, extrapolate from the past at your own risk. Plot a curve through the years 1917 to 1990 and what happened in Russia in 1991 isn't even on the same chart.

The professional military analysts added Vietnam to the Iran-Iraq War and foresaw tens of thousands of American casualties in the gulf. The professional arms controllers foresaw us painfully inching to a safer world by debating whether a missile originally deployed with seven warheads might count as three; within the space of a few months, a lifetime's worth of studies and formulas had been replaced by the question of how nuclear weapons can be disposed of as fast as the politicians declare them obsolete.

The professional doomsayers foresaw the world's dying a thousand deaths (a short sampling: starvation, toxic waste, global warming, global cooling) as the trends of the past continued unbroken into the future; the "massive famines" that overpopulation guru Paul Ehrlich warned were "certainly" to occur in the last decade have, in his latest pronouncements, apparently been postponed.

As Tom Peters has repeatedly stated of the business community, the only constant is change. Yet, I am certain that even Mr. Peters was not prepared for the cataclysmic change pouring over the world today. We are clearly living in a difficult time. Having traveled the world many times in the last several years as Chief Executive Officer of multi-national companies, and now as Chief Executive Officer of Mail Boxes Etc., I can tell you that the business community world-wide has never seen anything like this before. All of the rules are being re-written.

At home, we are plagued by rising debt, growing civil, racial and ethnic hatred, disintegrating moral values, sexually transmitted diseases and AIDS. Lost jobs, broken lives, ruined careers, bankruptcies, and shattered marriages have invaded our homes. It's as if some nameless, shapeless dread presages the end result of both moral and spiritual bankruptcies in our society.

The entire world is in turmoil and the political and social and cultural transformations stagger the imagination. We should not be surprised to see fraud, corruption and abuse at every level of society. A deep well of resentment seems to be winnowing its way into the hearts of many people and deep within the soul of our society there is a sickness that seems to bear the stamp of destiny.

As Mark Helprin said in a speech at Hillside College, "What does it matter if I break the links between action and consequence, work and reward, crime and punishment, merit and advancement? I myself cannot imagine a military threat (and never could) so what does it matter if I weld shut the silo latches on our ballistic submarines? What does it matter if I would shut my eyes to weapons of mass destruction in the hands of lunatics who are building long range missiles? Our jurisprudence is the envy of the world so what does it matter if I perjure myself, a little? What is an oath? What is a pledge? What is a sacred trust?

There appears to be a psychic and intellectual laziness that has seduced contemporary attitude.

Neither sermons on chastity nor demonstrations on how to roll on a condom are going to solve the AIDS crisis. For acquired immune deficiency syndrome is only one exacerbating symptom of a troubled mankind. Why are the children obsessed with sex and drugs and having things? Where are their fundamental values, their ambitions, their romantic longings and idealistic goals?

Why has violence in society become so pervasive that it seeps into the lunchroom and playgrounds? Have the rules failed, or did we fail them?

When did parents lose their grip? Or did they just let it go?

What happened to productive work? Why do we spend so much time chasing other people's money?

When did living lose a higher purpose? And why have we lost faith in the future?"

Beverly Sills in a speech commented, "Our kids-and we as well-are relentlessly and systematically desensitized to almost every form of disgusting behavior. Youngsters think that freedom means doing your own thing, and because we have set no standards for them and have given them no proper sense of values, the lowest common denominator of human behavior doesn't shock them. Their responsibilities and obligations to their fellow human beings simply are not being taught to them. A civilization rises on the strength of its values, and what we are talking about here are values. Lost values." Consider the following reports over the last three years about lost children with lost values.

November, 1996: A teenage girl delivers a child in a Delaware motel, then she and her boyfriend allegedly put the living baby in a plastic bag and drop it in a dumpster.

April, 1997: According to police, a young girl in Brooklyn wraps her newborn in plastic and leaves it to suffocate in a dresser drawer.

June, 1997: A New Jersey teenager gives birth to her baby in a bathroom stall at her high school prom. She drops the baby in the trash, then returns to the dance floor, where she and her boyfriend ask the band to play their favorite song, *The Unforgiven*.

September, 1997: A young Michigan woman gives birth to a daughter, then allegedly tosses her out with the trash. The following day, the dead baby is discovered in the jaws of a neighborhood dog.

October, 1997: A 16-year old boy in Pearl, Mississippi, allegedly slays his mother, then goes to school and shoots nine students, killing three and wounding five of his classmates.

December, 1997: A 14-year old boy in Stamps, Arkansas, allegedly fires sniper rounds outside his school, wounding two students.

March, 1998: Denver residents watch while a cab driver is beaten to death by four teens.

What we need is a return to basics. Eugene H. Methvin, a CPA and Vietnam veteran, who placed his career and reputation on the line to expose how our nations major colleges were bilking the American taxpayers out of millions of dollars said, "I think God is looking for a lot of little people to get America back on the straight and narrow."

Dr. Jack Graham, Pastor of the Prestonwood Baptist Church in Dallas, Texas, tells the story of a man who was trying to read the evening paper while his young son kept pestering him with questions. Finally, in exasperation at not being able to read, he took an advertisement from the paper that had a picture of the world on it and, tearing it in pieces, he told his son to go and put the world back together and then they would play a game. Anticipating he would have peace and quiet for at least a half hour, he was quite surprised when his son came running back in ten minutes with the picture of the world in perfect order. Quite astounded he asked his son to explain the speed of his success. Daddy, he said, there was a picture of a man on the other side and when I put the man back together, then the world was all right. That is what this book is about. Not looking to others to fix our problems but coming face to face with personal accountability. Not attempting to put the world together first, but first putting ourselves back together.

Unfortunately, the world is already too filled with how to books, how to guides, seminars and cassettes dispensing the secrets of success that are really not secrets at all. The last thing we need is another set of principles exhorting us to accumulate wealth, or make it big, or how to restore our self esteem. The truth is we seldom pay attention to columns of instructions, regulations or laws, no matter how important they are. Consider the most important guide for living ever received, The Ten Commandments! Even these are ignored. Less than half of all Christians that piously profess to believe them can recite more than five.

Moreover, it is overwhelming when you reflect on the tomes of literature available and all the speeches given and all of the instruction made pertaining to keys to health, wealth, success and life itself. And still we continue to run from our restlessness and a sense of incompleteness while vital truth that penetrates the core issues of life is replaced with a technical truth that allows people to compete academically and professionally but obviates deep communication where the real questions go wanting for an answer. Why do the philosophers, psychologists, theologians and such modern day purveyors of truth as songwriters, film makers and novelists rarely answer the hard questions? All of us need help. Clearly something is wrong. Whatever the path, it ought to touch the confusion of people's lives and offer patterns of living that are real to people who long for life. People that want happiness and peace of mind. People who want to make a lasting difference and long for impact. People who want to focus but simply don't know where to turn. We need the truth spoken without equivocation.

Many years ago, C.S. Lewis posited that man has always known the difference between right and wrong and that selfishness has never been admired. In fact, he called it a law of nature that man believed in decency and was inclined to behave in that way. I don't believe this is the case in America or in American business today. This rule of right and wrong may no longer apply. What Lewis says that may still be true is that men find themselves under a moral law, which they did not make and cannot quite forget, even when they try. We are in serious trouble in America and we are going down the wrong road. What I have observed in the business world these past years is only a reflection of the same disease that troubles our country and perhaps the world. The buzz word in business today is FOCUS and that is exactly what we need to do. We need to return to the basics and FOCUS on a few fundamental issues; fair play, unselfishness, courage, good will, faith, honesty, trust, integrity, truthfulness are all examples of the types of precepts upon which we need to focus. I believe we are learning that this cannot be done by legislation or ideologies that are already leading us to the brink of Armageddon. Good men and women cannot be legislated into law and you cannot have a good country without good men and women. The futility of our present worldly burden speaks for itself. As the Reverend Billy Graham says in his book *Storm Warnings*"...deepening poverty, racial division, homelessness, crime, physical and sexual abuse, and the breakdown of the traditional family. Our confidence has been shocked by scandals in the church, in government, in education, and at every level of authority. We have seen pictures of police officers beating citizens and top government officials and business leaders convicted of cheating and lying and fraud. We have seen moral and religious leaders, men who claim to be followers of Jesus, fall into disgrace in the eyes of God and men. We have seen the word of God distorted by false teachers to accommodate the slide in morals and values. Nothing positive can spring forth from the soil of despair."

Some have said that this generation may be the most critical in history. Civilization is surely shaking. Others like Francis Hayakawa, a former U.S. Department policy planner, have even predicted, with democratic pluralism having triumphed, the end of history. We need help for our children. We need help for ourselves. We need help in business and in government and at every level of society.

"Easy morals and promiscuity lead inevitably to disappointment, despair and death. History declares this tragic legacy of promiscuous society from Carthage and Rome to Renaissance France. In our search for absolute freedom from moral restraint or personal responsibility, many believe they can pay for their sins with cash. Everywhere you look you see TV news reports, radio bulletins, saying the world is in chaos and that no one has a solution. Violence, abuse, unhappiness, unrest in the cities, economies gone mad, the world seeks hope and what we get are charlatans, pop psychologists, educators, social scientists, physicians and wizards of all kinds offering quick trip remedies that fail. The hopeless end instead of the endless hope." Yet, there are still great enterprises to serve, great thoughts to think and great deeds to accomplish. If life, as Mohandes Ghandi once reflected, is a continual sifting of values and priorities, and our life's time and energy are limited, What are we then to do?

There is an answer. However, while simple, it is not easy. It involves reversing the very process that got us where we are. We are at the crossroads. We must individually and collectively utilize the greatest power that God has given us...the power to choose. We must decide where we are going to focus. This is not someone else's choice, it is ours, yours and mine. For in the end, it will be this choice that dictates our destiny, individually and as a country. **Focus on the fundamentals.**

James H. Amos, Jr.

"He that troubleth his own house shall inherit the wind."
"Where there is no guidance, the people fail . . . ."

-Solomon

I

AT THE CROSSROADS

The late W. Edwards Deming shortly before his death, wrote that "we have reached the limits of the capability of our current philosophy and resulting methods of management. American industry, our services, our government and our education are today in an invisible prison. The walls of this prison are the basic assumptions that are made today about economics and human behavior. They are outmoded in the global economy of this day. We can emerge from this prison only through knowledge that is not a part of the present system"...Deming goes on to point out that the cost of mistrust allocated to business and society, as a result of this situation to the Western world cannot be measured. Without trust there cannot be cooperation between people, teams, departments, divisions. To Deming this means transformation of the individual. I would submit that he is exactly right except that the limits of our current philosophy and resulting methods of management can be overcome by looking to traditional values and mastering fundamentals that we once embraced as opposed to attempting to create something outside the present system that never existed before.

The key to restoring the good of the past is to unlock the past, retrieving what worked from those who came before.

William Bennett has done that in his best seller, *The Book of Virtues*. He writes of the time-honored task of morally educating the young: "Moral education - the training of heart and mind toward the goal - involves many things. It involves rules and precepts - the dos and don'ts of life with others - as well as the explicit instruction, exhortation and training. Moral education must provide training in good habits. Aristotle wrote that good habits formed at youth make all the difference."

Our youth are forming bad habits, and our culture, through its music, movies, television and divorced or overworked parents, is infesting them with demons that no speech by a president and no amount of money can exorcise.

Today, there seems to be awakening in America and the world, an aversion to systems, governments, patterns of living and lifestyles that have not brought peace of mind, happiness and well-being to life. Everywhere we hear plaintive cries for a return to a simpler time. On January 16, 1990, *Parents Magazine* began this decade by reporting that 78% of the respondents wanted to return to traditional values and old-fashioned morality. The idea seemed to be that if we could just go back to what was, perhaps things would be much better. It is this search for what is often referred to as basics or fundamentals that is the core of our journey. The question is then begged, exactly what are these fundamentals we must master? On what should we focus our attention?

It appears that one of the consequences of so much instruction from so many different sources is that lines have been blurred pertaining to basics and fundamentals. Particularly, as they pertain to such things as values, love, leadership, relationships, forgiveness and other equally powerful concepts. It is possible, that things might be more simple than they are made to appear. I am well aware that I may be excoriated by certain deep thinkers and philosophers but I would like you to consider that, at least at some point in life, you and I really do know the difference between right and wrong and good and evil. C.S. Lewis was right in that without attending complicated courses on ethics, there is something inside each one of us letting us know there are few redeeming qualities associated with rape, murder, theft and other equally reprehensible acts. In a very simple sense, it seems that many people are yearning to return to a time when we knew that we had done wrong because we felt badly. Unfortunately, the triggers that indicated this insight seem to be disappearing.

Seventy years ago Oswald Spengler chilled the intelligentsia of Europe by predicting the "yellow races" would overrun Europe. Later, Arnold Toynbee would agree with him but offer what could only be described as a wildly improbable cure: "a spiritually oriented world society." If that were grasping at straws in the 1930's, it would appear to be even more remote today.

Alistair Cooke once reflected on his reluctance to write a piece entitled *"Whither America?"*[4] Is America in decay? Cooke states, the etiology of decadence has remained much the same over the past 200 years, and Gibbon's diagnosis of the symptoms are still the most persuasive: "1. The injuries of time and nature. 2. The hostile attacks on the barbarians and the Christians. 3. The use and abuse of the materials. 4. The domestic quarrels of the Romans." Gibbon's fourth cause, decay from within, is reflected in our own anxieties today. Cooke further writes, "I do not remember a time, not even during the ghastly 60's, when Americans have complained more, in a tone close to despair, about the visible and seemingly unhealable wounds in American society." He feels this is evidenced across America and cites two cultural symptoms that drive his conviction: 1. The abuse of liberty - through the far-flung and preposterous exploitation of the First Amendment to sanction any form of conduct, 2. The failure of the courts, including the Supreme one, to define and constrain obscenity.

Could it be that we have absorbed so much relativistic teaching that there are very few absolutes left. Perhaps, as Ghandi indicated, we should re-examine our values. Is there anything left that we hold absolutely sacred? Harry Emerson Fosdick once mused that everything rests back on integrity. That the driving power in life was personal character. Is it possible that the log wood of our lives is rotten? As we try to carve out our future should we ask ourselves if it is possible to carve rotten wood?

How can a doctor who misdiagnoses the disease effectively suggest a remedy? We listen to the gurus and thinkers, many of whom are enriching themselves at our expense, by telling us what we want to hear. And, more often than not, this has nothing to do with reality or the fundamental reality that begins and ends with us. We need a renewed sense of social responsibility. Many of our problems are simple, a consequence of unwise choices of behavior and lifestyle: we need a return to old-fashioned virtues and self-discipline, integrity and taking responsibility for one's actions. What we really need is moral leadership. To examine the result of instruction is to observe the result of application. How can a stream rise higher than its source? How can a painter create beyond his or her own capacity to create? If we are going to really master fundamentals, we must start with us. If we really want to focus on the basics then we have to go back to the beginning. You and I cannot change results by changing our environment or circumstances any more than the physician can cure the disease by treating the symptoms. We must once again embrace personal responsibility and accountability. This is not a black, white, hispanic or any kind of racial issue. This is about leadership. We desperately need leaders who are willing to champion and model this teaching. In business, systems, process or management technique is no surrogate for leadership. The leader embues the vision and does it with constancy of purpose. Have you asked yourself lately what is the purpose of America? Have you asked yourself what the vision for America is and who is defining it? A vision must permeate an organization's goals and policies.

Americans who once worshiped in the church of self-reliance have moved to another house of worship whose propagandists insist upon respect without accomplishment.

All of us, including the most damaged, would be helped by a moratorium on self-pity. We need less adolescent posturing and more stoic maturity; less weeping and gnashing of teeth and more bawdy horse laughing in the face of adversity.

In the cities of America, the young are being introduced to the world through the shaping ideology of victimism...self-esteem, instead of self-discipline, has become part of our educational creed. Teachers, parents and employers accept mediocre performance so as not to injure precious egos. Our children are not materially poor; however, they are spiritually impoverished. They've been led to believe that life's disappointments and challenges are violations of human rights; gratification is never to be postponed; ethics and values depend on the person and the situation; and honesty and morality are only for chumps. Not all youngsters have this vision of the world, but enough have it so that the future stands in jeopardy.

It is difficult to play the game without knowing the rules. If we do, we must recognize that even if we don't know the rules when we break them there are still consequences. Could it be that this is the reason that there is still so much heartbreak and pain after so much instruction. Quick fix techniques, looking out for number one, power strategies, communication skills, the gospel of positive thinking all may be essential but they are certainly not primary. If the foundation upon which these and other applications rest is weak, what can the result be but still more heartbreak, disappointment, pain and failure. A flawed character, duplicity, insincerity, lack of truth all indicate that the starting point, the real essentials are malformed. Only basic goodness gives life to the style and techniques we choose to apply to life. There are no short cuts. The price must be paid every day. It is the law of the harvest that you and I reap what we sow in our behavior and in all human relationships. The bankrupt morals we reflect in America today are a consequence for our personal failure to focus on what is right. Once again, it becomes a matter of priorities and values. Without deep integrity and character strength, relationships fail. When relationships fail, organizations fail. When relationships fail, systems fail. Organizations do not get better, people do. Countries don't get better, people do. Systems do not work by themselves, people work systems.

"Our country is in trouble. We have problems with productivity, standard of living and work ethic. Families are disintegrating. Our streets have become drug-war zones. Our classrooms are turning out thousands of functionally illiterate and morally bereft young people. Our economy is in a shambles and our government deliberately keeps millions of people idle while our work force produces second-rate products while demanding first rate benefits. Something is wrong. Fewer and fewer Americans want to work or take pride in what they do. Five million people live in permanently subsidized unemployment while welfare rolls continue to swell. Our crime rate is the highest in the world. Something is very wrong. What happened to the heritage of our forefathers of industry, thrift, diligence and respect for property. Somehow we have destroyed the sense of individual dignity and purpose of our people. Russia exemplified a society that was sick at heart. Where people walked the streets in dejection and despair. A society riddled with crime and where suicide had become a natural form of escape. A society suffering from the advanced stages of what the Danish philosopher Soren Kierkegaard called "soul sickness." The world is now seeing the bankruptcy of socialism. But what about America? Since 1969, average weekly earnings in constant dollars have fallen by more than 12 percent. More than half of today's young people leave school without the knowledge or foundation required to find and hold a job."[5]

What we need is action anchored in integrity in our leaders. We must become, once again, a people of honor, trust, integrity and commitment. It is hard to live up to an ill-defined standard. We must once again model excellence.

Everywhere we turn today, we are bombarded with terms that reference such things as a new world order, new age thinking, and even a new language that is to support this "growth" that exhorts us to keep an open mind and not be judgmental. In the middle of all this muddle, is an underlying attitude that prevents any discussion of right and wrong and good and evil. We retreat from making moral distinctions and spend our time discussing nothing. Yet, as professor Allen Bloom says in his book *The Closing of The American Mind*, Americans long for something lost – the great moral truths upon which our civilization rests. It is a longing for the kind of substance that gave such breathtaking meaning to the Declaration of Independence in which men pledged "our lives, our fortunes, and our sacred honor." Education, Bloom asserts, is not merely about facts – it is about truth and "the state of our souls." The great classics of life were once studied to help find answers to the meaning of life and to illuminate the struggle between right and wrong. In the past, students arrived at universities with an educational heritage rooted in the Bible, the family and an American political tradition centered on the Declaration of Independence. The Bible was a common culture that united the simple and the sophisticated, the rich, the poor and the young and old. And, Bloom notes that the family was the true seat of religious teaching resulting in a simple faith that had respect for learning. However, the product of recent ambiguous and relativistic teaching are students who are genuinely puzzled by such stories as *Romeo and Juliet* (why don't they just go live together?), the jealousy of *Othello* (he should go get some therapy), or the adultery (what's that) of *Anna Karenina*. They unthinkingly embrace a blind tolerance in which they consider it "moral" never to think they are right because that would mean someone else is wrong.

To move, let alone rout out the dead weight of all of this relativism will take an intellectual and spiritual assault of heroic proportions. I

17

believe that America and Americans long and ache for this. A return to a simple and rational way of speaking and thinking that is both easy to articulate, immediately comprehensible and powerfully persuasive. These are the real fundamentals that we must re-learn and re-master. They are waiting to be awakened in all of us. Perhaps beginning to consider these basics once again or provoking ourselves to think about these fundamental issues could be the real new beginning; a national paradigm shift that begets a true new world order that is affected at the source. A new foundation manifesting itself in eternal truths made strong by focusing on doing the right thing.

"Why is it that in the 1770's with only three million Americans we produced such leaders as Thomas Jefferson, Benjamin Franklin, George Washington, John Adams, James Monroe, James Madison and others while in 1998 with a population of over 250 million, it appears leaders go wanting. Could it be that what these early Americans were taught had a direct bearing on their performance and ultimate accomplishments? Interestingly, in the 1770's over 90% of our educational thrust was aimed at teaching moral values. By 1926, moral training was relegated to 6% and by 1990 it is not measurable. Yet, 91% of today's CEO's list integrity as their number one asset and their family as their number one priority. They are also people of faith."[6]

In the July 12, 1998 Editorial Section of the *San Diego Tribune*, it was pointed out that a bipartisan citizen's organization calling itself the National Commission on Civic Renewal headed by William Bennett and Sam Nunn had just completed a two year study. Amongst their findings was that the quality of America's civic life had declined by 40% since 1960. Obviously, most Americans hardly need to be told that the frayed fabric of their country's civic life needs repairing, urgently. Violent crime, broken families, drug abuse, a debased popular culture, neglected children and assorted other social maladies all testify to the imperative requirement of rebuilding America's civic life.

Nor, we think, do most Americans need reminding that this civic renovation is largely beyond the ability of government to accomplish. Government, in fact, has often demonstrated a perverse, if unintentional, knack for making things worse. Misguided social policies, a welfare system that bred demoralizing dependence, poor law enforcement, permissive courts and failing schools are ills attributable to government. Obviously, if we (you and I) want to help make America a better place for all its people we had better get busy.

As John Bunyan described the Pilgrims at the gate of the Celestial City, not only were the well equipped and the naturally strong able to carry through to the end but also along with Great Heart, Valiant for Truth, Honest and Steadfast were Mr. Feeble Minded, Ready to Halt, Mr. Despondency and his daughter, Much Afraid. Mastery is in the journey, not the destination.

James H. Amos, Jr.

RECOMMENDED READING:

Slouching Toward Gomorrah: Robert Bork; Harper Collins Publisher
Pilgrim's Progress: John Bunyan

It is our attitude at the beginning of a difficult undertaking which, more than anything else, will determine its successful outcome.

-William James

Yesterday the greatest question was decided which ever was debated in America; and a greater perhaps never was, nor will be, decided among men.

A resolution was passed without one dissenting colony, that the United Colonies are, and of right ought to be, free and independent States.

-John Adams

II

FOCUS ON: ATTITUDE

Attitude is a choice. It is the fundamental upon which <u>all</u> of the basics of life rest. Our attitude is the greatest asset or the biggest liability that we have. Life wears the color of our attitude. Of attitude, effort and knowledge, attitude is clearly the linchpin. While many would agree that knowledge is the prerequisite to success and sustained effort the track it runs on, attitude is the fundamental upon which all success rests. All of the knowledge in the world will not overcome a bad attitude. All of the effort expended toward a worthy goal will not make up for a bad attitude. Each of the fundamentals upon which we will focus are first and foremost attitudes. In books, seminars and tapes, we learn such things as our attitude will determine our altitude and that our disposition will determine our position. But, just what exactly is attitude? How do we know if it is good or bad? If it is bad, how do we change it? If it is good, how do we improve it? How long does it take?

Our attitudes are made up of the thoughts and conclusions that you and I reach in life about ourselves and other people. Attitudes are not developed overnight. They take time to develop and they take time to change. The fact is, if we are blessed with long life, you and I will meet ourselves as an old person one day. That old person will be kind and gracious and understanding or wizened and dried up like a prune, appearing to have been weaned on a pickle. These kinds of people superciliously look over the top of their glasses, waiting not so patiently for a vacancy in the Trinity. Whether good or bad, none of us reach this point in life instantly. Little by little, like icicles that form on the eaves of your house during a winter freeze, are attitudes developed. If the water that freezes to form the icicle is clear and free from pollution, then the icicle itself becomes pristine and clear. But let a little dirt or mud foul the flow and the icicle becomes opaque or splotched and not very attractive. Such is the case with people and attitudes. In all my years in the military and the business world one thing is perfectly clear, attitude is more important that facts, more important than the past or the future, more important than failure or success. Attitude is greater than appearance, competence or tools and has the capacity to make or break any enterprise, deal, negotiation, alliance or circumstance. You and I cannot always control what happens to us but we can control our reaction to what happens to us and that is attitude.

Perhaps it would be helpful to understand the components of attitude. Attitudes are made up of three things. First of all, the thoughts we think. Second, our feelings. Third, our actions. Unfortunately, most discussions relating to attitudes only address the first level or the cognitive. Consequently, no lasting improvement is made and real understanding of attitude development is lost. Instead, we are left to self contemplation and the oft heard admonishment that "we have an attitude," its implications, of course, that if we do, it must be bad. Let's take a few moments and look at each element of an attitude.

COGNITIVE: OUR THINKING

Most of our lives are lived in the mental not the tangible. Our thoughts can alter our lives because what we project at the center of our being is what we receive at the center of our situation. Many thinkers and educators have commented on this. Emerson said, "The key to every man is his thoughts." Marcus Aurelius said, "The world in which we live is determined by our thoughts." William James the father of American psychology once commented that the greatest discovery of his life was that his thoughts could change his future. Solomon commented over 2000 years ago, "As a man thinketh in his heart so is he," or it is not just the future but the present that is affected by our thoughts. The most significant discovery of my own life is that what we habitually think is our future. Our happiness depends on the quality of our thoughts. Unfortunately, most people seek temporary relief and not permanent victory. We live in the future hoping things will be different or in the past wishing things were the way they were. We must be able to look forward with confidence and backwards with no regret.

There are those that feel thoughts are creative forces and that since prayers are also thoughts, what is formed in the heart and spoken by the mouth has creative power. One thing is certain, and that is, that the deepest desire of our heart is what we accept in life. In that sense, there is no question that our thoughts are makers and creators. What we think about often enough, we do. The master weavers of our world are the thoughts we allow to go to seed. We become what we are by what we think. Like that old person you and I will meet someday, our condition is not by accident. Thoughts are taken at the high moment in life, like little children, hoping to be accepted and loved, given encouragement and guidance. The basic goodness of the thought or its inherent evilness makes no difference because what we mentally embrace over time ultimately becomes a common denominator in our life. Dreams, goals, values, choice, leadership, relationships, forgiveness, love, time, death, family, hope and other fundamentals are at their deepest, first attitudes. It may follow then that it is not what we are that holds us back in life it is what we think we are not. We can verbally confess goals and objectives, love, hope and many other things. But if at the very center of our being we are mentally rejecting what we confess, if our thoughts are uncommitted or scattered, if we think only failure, defeat and discouragement, then that is what we accept in life. I believe that when Jesus said that if a man lusts in his heart it was as if he had committed the act, he was reflecting on the power of thought gone to seed. That what we allow to take root in our imagination may become an imbedded belief or attitude that is so powerful that it deceives our own subconscious to the point where we can no longer differentiate between reality and imagination. C. S. Lewis said it another way, "If you look upon ham and eggs in lust you have already committed breakfast in your heart." Ultimately, the common denominator of our thoughts, good or bad, what we dwell on most of our days does become reality in our life. No thought can be kept a secret. It crystallizes into an image in the mind and molds the body into an expression of that image. The incredible impact and power of our thinking and its affect on our lives is monumental. And yet, we spend very little time considering what we allow to enter our minds or still, more importantly, what we choose to dwell on or allow to take form and substance in our minds. Chances are we would become much more agitated by someone throwing garbage on our living room rug than we would by the garbage that we allow to funnel daily through our ears to our minds and hearts and ultimately to our behavior. Dag Hammarskjold wrote in *Markings*, "You cannot play with the animal in you without becoming wholly animal, play with falsehood without forfeiting your right to truth, play with cruelty without losing your sensitivity of mind. He who wants to keep his garden tidy doesn't reserve a plot for weeds." The Biblical admonition to think on whatsoever things are true, just, honest, pure and of good report may be some of the best advice that has ever been given. Yet, as powerful as our thoughts are, if we assume by simply changing our thinking we can alter an attitude, we are mistaken.

EMOTIVE: FEELINGS

Thoughts stir the emotions and the emotions stir the will. A thought that is combined with emotions and feelings is on its way to becoming a belief. Prejudice is learned in exactly this same way. No one is born hating. Interestingly enough, we are born feeling before we become thinkers. It is the power of emotions that bring commitment to thought. As an example, knowing becomes fondness which may ultimately become love. All reflecting a different kind of thought and a much deeper emotion or commitment. Knowing may also become disliking that may degenerate into hate, also reflecting different thinking and a different emotion that evokes a different response. The point is, we cannot think about anything very long without emotion or feelings playing a part. Thus, the admonition to be careful upon which thoughts we dwell becomes paramount. This is why true neutrality or indifference is in reality not possible. As I have learned in negotiating agreements all over the world, you and I lean to one side or the other on every issue. The difference may be slight but it is there and as feelings and emotions have an impact pertaining to a particular issue, so do the responses we emote in life. There is not a person you know, a cause you serve, an organization you belong to, that over a period of time has not been altered by the feelings or emotions you experience and the resulting actions you take. Consequently, thoughts become confirmed through our feelings and emotions. Yet, as powerful as this combination of thinking and feeling is in our lives, until they drive our behavior or actions they are not yet attitudes.

BEHAVIORAL: ACTIONS

Thoughts stir the emotions, emotions stir the will and the will stirs the body to action. Action then becomes the fruit of thought and feelings. Our behavior is always decreed by our basic attitude. Attitudes made up of our thoughts, feelings and actions are crucial to every other fundamental we will discuss. Only action reflects our real attitude. It is not what we say or think or even feel that determines results. It is ultimately what we do. We may say we have hope, or we may say we have faith, we may say that we love, but unless that translates into action supporting what we confess, then we possess a different reality and a different attitude and must come face to face with a loss of integrity. This alignment of thinking, feeling and acting supported by a foundation of strong values is what produces integrity. Until a person faces him or herself in this matter, they are doomed to live a life at cross purposes where part of them frustrates the rest of them. Stephen Covey in his fine book *The 7 Habits of Highly Effective People* describes this basic attitude as a paradigm. He goes on to say that a paradigm is a model or theory, a frame of reference or assumption. He explains that it is the way we see the world - not in terms of our visual sense of sight, but in terms of perceiving, understanding, and interpreting. He further explains that paradigms are maps and not the territories themselves. However, while Mr. Covey separates attitudes from paradigms, I believe they are the same. Our attitudes, and as a result our real behavior, are the mental maps by which we live. They encompass what we think, the way we feel and the way we act. Generationally they become the Zeitgeist of the age.

An attitude then is multi-level. It is cognitive, it is emotional and it is active. Attitudes are the result of lifetime conditioning. Our families, our schooling, our jobs, our spiritual experiences, all contribute to the way we view life. That is why our attitude is so important. Our behavior must be congruent with our thinking and feeling or we cannot maintain wholeness. We lose our integrity. I've often heard it said that once you have a dream the facts no longer make any difference. The truth is, once you have an attitude, the facts don't make any difference. Good or bad the result is self-induced. It is always our interpretation of what the facts are that we manipulate by the application of our attitude which determines what the results will be. Therefore, changing an attitude is difficult because attitudes reflect, at our deepest, who we really are. Attitudes encompass our perceptions and our most fundamental beliefs. Dag Hammerskjold said, "The longest journey is the journey inward." He was correct because it is there that the answers are alive and not memorized. Everyone has one dominant life principle that they live by. It is this basic attitude, the thread by which the tapestry of life is connected that we weave our future and that thread can be for good or evil. The most beautiful tapestry in the world viewed from the reverse side is a mass of meandering thread and confusion. Yet, the weave is held together and the beauty of the wool driven by the common denominator of the thread. When you reflect on people you know or well known people you know about, it is not difficult to determine what life principle they live by. The thread that dominates the tapestry of these lives is often very obvious even if viewed in reverse. The life principle of Jesus Christ was love. The life principle of Ghandi was peace. The life principle of Mother Theresa was service and compassion. Of Adolf Hitler and more recently Saddam Hussein one can only think evil, hatred and destruction. If you and I were able to take this journey inward to examine the life principle or basic attitude upon which we approach each day, we would not only be looking at the reality of the present, but into the face of the self- fulfilled prophecy of our future. And, as we will see later, we fear this deep inward look because most of us feel if we face it, it will ruin what little comfort we have. It is therefore imperative that we recognize the absolute of attitude. That attitude is multi-dimensional, made up of thinking, feeling and actions. That simply changing our thinking does not change an attitude. But rather, what we dwell on, what we allow to sink to an emotional level ultimately becomes action in our life. This is attitude. In fact, this is the basic premise of psychoneuorimmunology. That our thoughts and feelings affect the nervous system and that we can even alter the immune response of our bodies. I doubt there is anyone that doesn't know what AIDS is today. This tragic disease that destroys the body's immune system is epidemic. But, I wonder how many people have succumbed from

MIDS or what I would call mental immune deficiency syndrome where the body's immune system has been altered by destructive attitudes that resulted in emotional and sometimes physical destruction of our lives.

Extending from the brain is a four inch cord called the Reticular Activity System. This system filters incoming sensory stimuli and decides what stays. As we have seen, we will always move in the direction of our currently dominant thoughts. The brain has built in neural tendencies to structure its operations in the form of stored programs. A memory trace in the brain tissue records a habit of thinking. Once that trace is strongly imbedded, the brain deals with it instead of new data. Most of our conscious thinking is done in these whole thought units or mental patterns. They are mental sets. They are thoughts that have been emotionally imbedded much like rain eroding a hillside into the brain. These are the paradigms or attitudes of life. They may be liberating or they may imprison.

In Vietnam, in 1968 and 1969 with the United States Marines, we would sometimes come across Tiger Cages, a six foot by six foot bamboo cage that was used by the North Vietnamese to carry prisoners of war from location to location. Often, American prisoners of war would spend days, weeks and even months in one of these cages incarcerated by the North Vietnamese, unable to stand or stretch out physically becoming stunted and debilitated. Similarly, many people today are what I would call P.O.T., or POTTED. They are prisoners of thought. Not physically but mentally restrained. Subject to monorail thinking they have developed psycho-sclerosis or a strongly held expectation or mental set that leaves them mentally stunted and debilitated. What you and I must do is to develop the right mental sets or attitudes. This requires a change in thinking, a change in feelings, and a subsequent change in behavior. Can you see then, that habits, whether good or bad are simply attitudes in action. That to alter an attitude we must affect all three levels, the thinking, feeling and behavioral elements of an attitude.

Take smoking, as an example. Most smokers will tell you that their first cigarette was not a particularly satisfying experience. Yet, over time through spaced repetition, a habit was developed that was too weak to notice until it became too strong to break. We have become an addictive society. And addictions of every type that are not organic, find their roots in similar behavior. It is a paradox that while we want to be in control, we are confused. In an angry moralism, we often shout at others to shape up because we cannot tolerate in them what we refuse to admit lies within ourselves. Every action we take has its root in the thoughts and feelings that pre-date that action. Changing bad habits requires changing goals in life which is another fundamental we will later discuss.

Isn't it interesting that sociologists tell us nothing in life of any value is ever accomplished except through the head, the heart and the hands. Examining this idea further, all living things take on food first for sustenance, then for growth and finally to bear fruit. Ultimately, the thoughts we feed ourselves, allow to grow emotionally in our subconscious, result in action taken and later the fruit we bear in life. God help us not to be barren or worse yet, to produce pain, sorrow, discouragement and despair where there could have been joy and happiness and peace of mind.

A crisis is often described as anything that forces change. Permanent change is attitudinal. What we think, what we feel and what we do. If this is positive, the fruit of our lives may take on a beauty and pungency not previously there. It is our attitude that will determine the difference. Believing in limitations without testing them becomes a self-fulfilled prophecy. Remember that success is measured by what has to be overcome to get there and we all start at different places. Attitude becomes a bridge that will enable us to move from where we are to where we would like to be. If our attitude is right, our position is always temporary. This path we walk of attitudinal and habit change might be described as follows:

1. When we are wrong.

2. When we are wrong and know it.

3. When we are doing something about it.

4. When we change and no one believes it.

5. Respect of others and for ourselves.

This is clearly not a path of instant gratification. It does not pander to our societal demand for a three step solution to spiritual, mental and physical utopia. This is a process. There are no short cuts to our dreams. Consequently, there is often very little correlation between what we say we want and what we are willing to do to achieve it.

Real change then means change in the inner person. This is more than behavior modification. It is not the psychoanalytical application of the new age thinkers but the maturity of compassionate, enriching and penetrating relationships that have their roots in mature outlooks and attitudes. Again, attitude is multi-dimensional and impacts life in a like manner.

It is interesting to note -

ATTITUDE is made up of:

Thinking–Feeling–Acting

SOCIETY tells us everything of social value is done through:

Head–Heart–Hands

GOD chooses Himself to speak:

To us–In us–Through us

THROUGH life we are:

Melted–Molded–Strengthened

WE take food for:

Sustenance–Growth–To bear fruit

ULTIMATELY our:

Thoughts–Feelings–Control Destiny

The message is clear, if careful attention is not given to internal renewal, external improvement is hypocritical if not impossible. Something deep within us as individuals and as a nation requires change. If we do not change our thinking, our feelings, our actions - - - our attitude, we will continue to direct our lives and destiny based on our present understanding. If that understanding is wrong, it leads to death. Death of the individual and ultimately death of a nation.

When I first returned from Vietnam, I often had a dream where I stood in a long line of people clad in flowing robes with hoods shadowing their faces. I had the feeling that we all were trying to get to the head of the line to see who was leading and where they were going. It seemed that every time I made progress or was just at the point where I could reach the leader I would awaken. Life was also like that. Whether spiritually, mentally, or physically, every time I seemed to be making progress something would happen that would set me back. I never seemed to be able to get to the finish line. One night, after a particularly trying experience, the dream was recurring but this time I was able to pull the hood back on the leader and I came face to face with me. The message was, of course, it was not someone else leading me. It was not someone else determining the direction and the results, it was me. That hooded individual represented the mental set or attitude upon which I was approaching life. And so it is for you as well. It is not our circumstances that determines the results, it is our reaction to them. Consider this: The basic attitude and mental sets upon which we approach life, that common denominator, the thread that holds our life's tapestry together, not only determines what we are against but what we are for. Somewhere I once read the following:

1. You are following someone: Even if you insist you are following no one.

2. You believe something: Even if you insist that you don't believe in anything because believing in nothing is something.

3. You are living for something: Even if you are so busy making a living you don't know what you are living for.

4. You are going somewhere: Even if you have not bothered to get directions or decide on a destination.

5. You are becoming someone: Even though you may be so completely preoccupied with the present you ignore the future.

6. You've got a destiny: One way or another - even though you may be indifferent to it.

So, your attitude will determine:

1. Who you choose to follow.

2. What you choose to believe.

3. What you live for.

4. Where you are going.

5. What you are becoming

6. Your very destiny.

How much more fundamental can we possibly get? I exhort you to consider your attitude as we focus on life's fundamentals. It is the single greatest asset or liability that you possess. It is the foundation upon which you build. **Focus on attitude.**

RECOMMENDED READING:

As A Man Thinketh: James Allen

The Go Getter: Peter Kyne

Attitude - Your Most Priceless Possession: Chapman

I believe in America because in it we are free –
free to choose our government, to speak
our minds, to observe our different religions . . . .

Because we have great dreams –
and because we have the opportunity to make
those dreams come true.

-Wendell L. Willkie

There are those, I know, who will reply that
the liberation of humanity, the freedom of man and
mind is but a dream –

They are right–

It is the American dream.

- Archibald Macleash

III

FOCUS ON: THE DREAM

Everybody wants something. Cars, homes, peace of mind, happiness, recognition, a place to belong, the list is endless. Because of this, desire is at the foundation of all effort. It is from desire that persistence grows because what attracts you can activate you to action. It is this attraction or desire or dream, if you will, that is the beginning of faith. Faith is actually a reaction to a dream and dreams are God inspired. It is important to remember that God places no limitations on our dreams or achievements. Only we do that.

Developing this dream or vision and living it is one of the essential elements of leadership. It is this point of differentiation that will separate those people and organizations that succeed in the millennium from those that do not. It is also the point of differentiation that will determine the direction our country proceeds as well as our ultimate success. The dream predates the goal and all leadership begins and ends with goal setting. It is the dream that shows up and then shores up values. It creates energy and drives people to do what sociologists suggest is the prerequisite for all accomplishment, people working with their heads, their hearts and their hands. Behavior is not driven by experience but by expectation. Years of motivational programs for people in business have taught me "You get what you incent." If you don't like the results change the incentive and renew the dream. It is the dream that kindles the imagination and becomes a self-fulfilling prophecy. In *Proverbs 29:18*, it is written that "Where there is no vision, the people perish."

The dream not only predates goals, but it encompasses and transcends them inspiring people with a spiritual energy. Napoleon once said that the only way to lead people is to show them the future and the future is encompassed in the dream, pursued in faith and inspired in hope. This is why I would exhort you to get a new hold on your dream. This is why it is important for our country to get a new hold on our dream.

31

It is my observation that one of the essential elements of successful organizations is trust. Trust is not only at the heart of cooperative effort but it sustains that effort. Implicit within it is the ability to mold the individual into the collective, for what is formed in the heart has creative power. You cannot find the spirit of man by dissecting his heart or find his intellect by dissecting his brain. Nor can you find the power to grow an organization in its pro formas or its spread sheets. Motivation is at the heart of the matter and at the heart of the matter is the dream. Recognition, security, a place to belong, purpose and hope all reside in the dream. Get a new hold on your dream.

It is the dream that offers texture to life. While we cannot control the length of our life, we can add to its width and depth and breadth. Life inspired by a God-given dream is not a burden we carry, but wings that transport us to new heights providing us with a reason to live. We live in inspiration offered by the great dreamers of history. From them, we draw from one generation and are able to give to another. Dreams allow us to speak in a language that does not die a physical death. Dreams are the harbinger of hope and glory speaking in a language of the spirit, the heart and the soul. This is why it is so destructive to embrace a so-called political correctness that takes great delight in tearing down the traditions and dreams of the past. For, when the dream dies, there is no hope.

Communism, as an example, over time, proved to be as soulless as the embalmed remains of Lenin in Red Square, collapsing in the dust of a visionless society. No dream, no hope, no trust and no future. The people simply quit believing. The fundamentals you and I are discussing, love, forgiveness, relationships, attitude and dreams, simply sank into a morass of hopelessness. You and I must grasp the dream that brings out the best in us. Moving in the direction of our aptitudes and abilities, we must keep our eyes on our values, willing only to sacrifice the dream for the sake of our integrity. Seeing the dream through to the end is a function of dedication, determination, hard work and character. It is not, as our narcissistic self-centered society has determined, a divine right to embrace happiness, health and prosperity. Winners take what they have and make it better. They don't complain about the past or the tarnished dreams of their forefathers demanding the result without the effort. Further, they know that it is not what they get that makes them successful but rather what they become in the process and then what they continue to do with what they get. The journey is the issue and a fundamental sense of purpose is the single most important element in the journey. The objective of life then, is to run to the dream and not from the shadows. The greatest tragedy is to never have had a dream, not to fall short in achieving it, as some have said. Get a new hold on your dream.

I once heard writer and speaker, Doug Wead, tell the story of David and Goliath from the 17th Chapter of Samuel in the Old Testament. I would like to share that with you because it so typifies what we are discussing. Most children have heard the story of David and Goliath before but Doug told it from the standpoint of an adult. To some it may seem like he was violating sacred stories, but bear with me because as Doug says, "They don't teach it this way in Sunday School."

Let me set the stage for you. The Valley of Elah runs east and west from the Mediterranean Sea to just a few miles south of Jerusalem. The Philistine Army was on a mountain on one side of the valley and the Israeli Army was on a mountain on the other side of the valley. In the middle of the valley was Goliath, pacing up and down. It happens that Goliath and his brothers were a remnant of a giant race of people that had been left to test Israel in the settlement of Canaan or the Promised Land. Now Goliath was big. In fact, if you count a cubit as 25 inches and span as 10 inches, Goliath was 13 feet four inches tall. He was also wearing armor that weighed 194´ pounds troy and carried a spear of 23´ pounds troy. Translated, that means his total armor weighed 218 pounds. In Vietnam, a fully loaded combat Marine with full pack didn't have an average weight much more than Goliath's armor.

Now, David arrived in the Israeli camp that afternoon. As it happens, everybody was decked out for battle with flags waving and trumpets blaring and horses snorting. David was excited just to be able to watch. David was a spectator. Then, Goliath showed up. To me what is interesting about this, is that Goliath could be any obstacle between you and your career or between you and your mate or between you and financial goals or your children or the successful operation of your business or whatever. But for David, as we shall see, Goliath became the very best thing that could have ever happened to him. Goliath or the obstacle or problem became the beginning of a great career for David and it could be for you too. You want to do something with your life and sometimes Goliath problems get in the way, but they also bring out the very best in us. This is what happened in David's case.

When Goliath appeared, he gave a speech. The fact is, he gave that same speech for 40 days before David arrived and when Goliath spoke, all Israel ran, even David. We aren't taught that in Sunday School. When I was little I used to go to Vacation Bible School during the summer at a little Presbyterian Church near my house in Florissant, Missouri. It was there that I first saw a picture of David and Goliath stuck to a flannel board that was used to tell the stories of the Bible. However, I never saw a picture of David running away. What the flannel board showed was a picture of David standing his ground and saying, "Who is this uncircumcised Philistine?" Now, I don't think most kids know what circumcised means. I certainly didn't. I've often wondered how many children lived for years in mortal fear of anything that might be uncircumcised that could cause the whole army of Israel to run away. And all Israel did run. If you understand the military strategy of the day, the entire first row was prepared to die but even they ran away when Goliath showed up.

So, David was running as well. When he got back to camp he happened to overhear a conversation that was to change his life. Now, this is absolutely true and you can find it in the Bible, so I encourage you to look it up and check it out. Here is what happened. Two soldiers were talking and one said to the other, "Do you know what the reward is for the person that kills Goliath?" The other one responded, "Yes, if you kill Goliath you won't have to ever pay taxes again, you will be able to ride a great horse, and listen to this, you will marry the princess and become prince." Right here is where David said what they taught us in Sunday School as kids. "What?" "Who is this uncircumcised Philistine?" Here is the point. It wasn't Goliath or the problem that turned David on, it was the princess. It was the dream. David then said, "What" because he wanted it repeated and so they did. What this means is that you must have a vision, a dream and a goal.

David, as it turns out, was just like you and me. He wanted to do something with his life before he died. He tended his sheep and dreamed until one day the word prince caught his ear. The vision the Bible talks about when it says that you must have a vision or perish is the vision for your marriage, a vision for your career or your business or even a vision for your life. God tells us how important it is to have a dream all through the Bible. Remember the story of Joseph and his multi-colored coat? Joseph ended up going to prison and being made a slave and put in a pit. But God did not show him that. Instead, God looked down on this smart alec kid just as he does you and me and while Joseph was trying to impress his brothers with his new clothes, God gave him a dream. The Bible says that Joseph got up in the middle of the night and said, "Hey, I've had this wonderful dream, and in it all your haystacks were bowing down to my haystack." As you might imagine, his brothers didn't like that. In derision his brothers said of him, "behold the dreamer cometh." The truth is, nobody likes dreamers, especially if they don't have a dream of their own. This is why it is so important to protect your dream. If God gives you a dream don't let someone kill it; not even your brother or sister or parents or spouse who are often well-intentioned but simply don't understand.

The same thing happened to David, incidentally. David's brother Eliab walked up to the campfire and saw that David was impressing the soldiers. Now Eliab knew that David was a nobody. He knew that

David would never be a prince or ride a great horse or own land or certainly would never marry the princess. So Eliab said "OK, David, I know why you are here. You just wanted to see what the soldiers look like." Then Eliab said what was most devastating to David in front of the others. He said, "By the way, who is tending your few sheep?" Then, of course, the soldiers also realized David was a nobody too. You see, David was away from home. When you are home, everybody knows you are a nobody. Your relatives know you are a nobody, your friends know you are a nobody and you know you are a nobody. When you return home there are banners there that say welcome home nobody. Your spouse even has nobody embroidered on your bath towel and so you begin to believe it and to think it yourself. David was away from home and he didn't know he was a nobody. So, what did David do? The Bible says, that he turned from one to another. What this means is that he found someone else to listen to his dream that might agree with him. When he found someone else, it is interesting to note, that he asked the same question for the third time. "What is the reward for the man who kills Goliath?" What I like about David is that he puts his mind on the princess or the dream and not on the problem. Too many times in life we are absorbed with the problem. All you hear is Goliath, Goliath, Goliath. We become walking health problems. We join the arthritis book of the month club. We see only how our business will fail and never seem to grasp the fact that you don't drown by falling in the water, just by staying there. Instead, we seem to spend most of our lives preparing to fail.

Not David. By this time, he was walking all over the battlefield asking questions like, "What kind of perfume does she wear? How does it feel to ride a big horse? How much land do I actually get?" You see there is power in putting your mind on the reward. There is power in staying focused on the dream. You must have a vision. You must have a goal. You must have a dream. You must have a hope. So what did David do? According to the Scripture it says he actually began to rehearse what he was going to say to King Saul. He said, "I may be small but I killed a bear and God will help me kill this guy." And so, as Doug Wead pointed out, David probably showed up in room 319 where everyone that was interested in killing Goliath was supposed to sign up and nobody was there. He probably thought, "Oh no, I'm late and they already picked the guy and I didn't even get the newsletter saying who it was." David was so worried about the competition and the other people that might want to marry the princess that he couldn't believe it when no one showed up. The fact is there wasn't anybody in line because they were all at home where they were nobody. It seems that when you get right down to it, no one wants to become a prince. No one wants to ride the big horse. No one wants to own the land. No one wants to marry the princess. And, most of all, NO ONE WANTS TO PAY THE PRICE. Is it possible that this is part of what ails America today?

No one wants to stay the course. No one wants to be accountable. No one wants to pay the price to achieve the dream.

So, first you must have a dream and then you have to try. Most of you already know that David won. But I do want you to remember that Goliath wasn't just big, he was a champion. When he was in the fourth grade his teacher probably went to the principal and said, "Look at that guy in the third row." And that was all it took. They took this freak of nature, a giant, and made him a champion. Goliath also had a dossier on the 36 great men of Israel. Like many great military leaders, he studied his opponents and he was ready. The plan was one Philistine for one Israelite. On the first day, a half million Israelis ran, the plan was so devastating. Goliath already knew who he might fight and when David showed up he probably thought to himself, "Now I see, they knew they would lose so they planned a propaganda reverse by sending a 17 year old boy." Then he said, "Am I a dog that you send a boy to fight against me? Send me a man." Obviously, Goliath had this inferiority complex to match his size. All his anger and paranoia came to the surface. I mean this guy was a freak. He couldn't even buy his shoes at K Mart like you and me. The really interesting thing is how David answered him. I wish that you would take the time to look this up in the Bible because it is really dynamite. You can find this in 1st *Samuel XVII, 45-47*. Here is what David said, "Thou comest to me with a sword and a shield and a spear but I come to you in the name of the Lord of Hosts, the God of the armies of Israel whom you have defiled." Remember the scene. There are a half million soldiers watching and this living legend was standing in front of David, all 13 feet 4 inches toting 218 pounds troy of armor. How was David armed? David came armed with a dream. He had a shepherd's staff, five smooth stones, a bag, a sling and faith in God. So David says, "This day the Lord will give you into my hand, and I will take your head from thee...(talk about faith, remember, he only had a sling shot).

Then David took one of his smooth stones and put it in the sling and slung it out there and hit Goliath in the one place that he wasn't covered by armor and Goliath fell.

AND THERE WAS SILENCE.

David stood there looking pretty cool on the outside like he might be saying, "pretty good shot, huh?" On the inside he was wondering if he had to go up and see if Goliath was dead. So he went and climbed up on Goliath taking his sword and severed his head. Then he knew he was dead. The Bible then says that all half million Israelites gave a great shout. HEY! Three days earlier they had all run away. Now, the Philistines ran because one boy had a dream and decided he wanted to be somebody. A prince and not a shepherd.

Many years later, as recorded in *Chronicles 28:20*, David was on his death bed. He was talking to his son Solomon and he wanted to leave him with just the right words. He wanted to imprint his life with his dying words. While you may not believe it, and again I encourage you to look it up, David's dying words reflected the attitude of his life and the commitment to the dream. David's dying words to his son Solomon were, "BE STRONG, BE OF GOOD COURAGE, AND DO IT!"

Life is not as easy as self-help books or the panderers of positive thinking suggest. It is often full of boredom and drudgery to the point where we may become overtaken by the ordinariness of life itself. It is full of wrong choices and failed dreams embraced by executives, street people, farmers, addicts, the famous and the ordinary. All the battles are still faced daily. Battles with lust, greed pride, anger, irritability and inconsistency. The life of the paradoxical encompassing both belief and doubt, hope and discouragement, love and hate. But in the dream is the power of the oasis. It offers renewal of the ebbing spirit. The thirst quenching water that offers respite in the middle of the desert, the strength to go on to a new day. With a new dream you are not 35 going on nowhere or a disillusioned old person that may soon die. God is a God of new beginnings and it is He that authors the dream. We may be discouraged, uncertain and guilt-ridden but there is hope. Within the dream lie the answers to our ultimate purpose and values. Within the dream lie the answers to the pain often caused by those closest to us. Yes, there is death, yes, there can be panic, yes, there is disillusionment, yes, there is sometimes depression but that is not all. At each moment in life we are growing into something more meaningful or retreating into something less than we are. Like everything else, the dream is a gift. We must allow our dreams to soar and not become empty, petty and impotent in the manure of this world. You and I need to think big about God and think big about our dreams. The energy, faith and devotion which we bring to the dream will light up our country and perhaps the rest of the world. Set your heart on things above as the dream is the substance of every great achievement. Just as water seeks its own level, our lives rise and fall based on the power of the dream. We all have a dream or vision that corresponds to our basic attitude about life. It gives definition to our very life, influencing the decisions we make, our choices, the words we speak, the feelings we express, and the actions we take. At any given time these actions either conform to the dream or they do not. This is a matter of integrity. The problem with America and many Americans today is that we have failed to maintain our integrity.

The dream is vital to life because it provides constant hope. It keeps us true. It keeps us from constantly looking at the other guy as the one who is fulfilled. Instead of regretting yesterday and fearing tomorrow, we have hope. In law, there is a concept referred to as "the covenant of good faith and fair dealing." This says that anything that might not be covered under the terms of the written contract between two parties will be covered under this covenant. That is exactly what the dream does. With the dream, God says to you and me in a covenant of good faith and fair dealings that there is a new purpose in life. With the dream, I know that out of despair comes hope...every time. With the dream I know, that out of the ashes rise the phoenix...every time. With the dream, I know that out of the wreck I rise...every time. Remember this, it is OK to commit your life to great and soaring dreams in your own imperfection. Over and over we have said that this is a journey we are taking not a destination. A perfect life is not the issue...what is demanded is a dedicated heart. Get a new hold on your dream.

Keep the dream in your heart alive, never let it go.

Keep the dream in your heart alive, faith can make it so.

God has plan'd so much ahead using you and me.

Keep the dream in your heart alive, never let it go.

-Anonymous

Focus on the dream.

RECOMMENDED READING:

Make Your Dream Come True: Chuck Swindoll

Life Is Tremendous: Charlie Jones

Over The Top: Zig Ziglar

*The American people can have anything they want;
the trouble is, they don't know what they want.*

- Eugene V. Debs

*The tragedy of the world is that
men have given first class loyalty
to second class causes and
these causes have betrayed them.*

- Lynn Harold Hough

IV

FOCUS ON: GOALS

Life appeals to us from innumerable directions. We tend to litter our lives with the indiscriminate, letting first come first served, forgetting that the finest things in life do not crow. In lock step with the old saw that the squeaky wheel gets the oil, we let the loudest voices fill our ears forgetting that asses bray but that gentlemen speak with moderation. We forget that it requires an engineer, an architect and a builder to construct a barn but that any jackass can kick one down. Like cue balls on a bumper pool table, we move from crisis to crisis, never really in control, leading not bad lives but lives frittered away on the inconsequential.

The first sign of maturity in a young person is when they begin to move in a determined manner toward a preset goal. In fact, ultimately, all leadership begins and ends with goal setting. Personal power is a product of its application. And, while setting goals does not guarantee success in life, not setting goals will almost assuredly result in failure. The point is, if you are not now making the progress you want to make it may be because your goals are not clearly defined. It is here where we choose to remain in mediocrity or rise above the average and move ahead of our time.

You and I must set goals in every area of our life. Spiritually, mentally and physically, like the legs on a three-legged stool each area is of extreme importance. Consequently, because we are limited in time, energy and resources, our values and priorities become the most crucial problem we face. Any business person worth his or her salt will take a yearly inventory of assets. A continual sifting of values and priorities is like that. This enables us to determine what our purposes in life should be. From our purposes, spring our goals. There is a difference between a purpose and a goal. A purpose might be to become a better father or mother. A goal supporting that purpose may be to spend time with our children or to offer them more guidance and counsel about the books they read and the friends with whom they associate. A purpose might be to become a better person. A goal supporting that purpose might be to devote more time to relationship building through compassion, forgiveness and understanding. When I was little, my father, who has a great tenor voice, used to sing to me. The words of one of the songs he sang taught me that "life was like a mountain railroad" with hills and tunnels along the way, with your hand upon the throttle and your foot upon the brake...Life is like that. Our life's purpose might be described as that train with one determined destiny that stops for friends, family, possessions, love...or the many goals that are significant enough to catch our attention along our chosen track. Whether they stop us or spur us on, they are still goals. Remember, it is <u>our</u> hand on the throttle and <u>our</u> foot on the brake. Sometimes, because of unfocused goals and indecision, we travel many miles in confusion trying to override the brake by pouring on more coal –we progress but haltingly. Outside of man there is not an idle atom in the universe. Everything is working out its mission. Only man can choose to be without purpose, live without meaning and die in insignificance! The inevitability of the track is old age and death. The value, priority and power of the goals or stops along the way cannot be overestimated. While we cannot control the length of our life, the track our train is running on, we can control its other dimensions; its breadth, its depth, its height.

I think you can see then that purposes are much broader in nature than goals, possibly requiring a lifetime to achieve. Goals, on the other hand, are more short term and quantifiable. Thus, as we think through our values and priorities as well as our basic attitude toward ourselves, we can determine, first the direction we take and later the foundation upon which we rest our hopes, dreams and goals. One of the things we must learn is that the great is often achieved at the sacrifice of the lesser and that the best isn't, and good enough never is. That every decision we make is made at the sacrifice of something else in our lives. That a first rate dedication to second rate causes or majoring in minors is not the answer. That the way we are facing has a great deal to do with our destination. Life has no value unless something of value is its objective.

If you are seventeen years old, in the next ten years you will reach some statistical milestones. You will complete your education. You will probably leave home and get married. You will start your first job and more than likely switch jobs at least once. What are your goals as they relate to these events? If you are thirty seven years old, in the next ten years you will statistically reach the occupational peak in your life. Your income will reach its maximum level and your children will be reaching college age and leaving home. Your body will be aging more rapidly and you will probably have less energy and endurance. You will be well on your way to middle age. What are your goals as they relate to these events? For many, preoccupation becomes the most common form of failure. There is a plethora of books and tapes that can instruct you about how to set short-term, intermediate and long-term goals. There are many programs, seminars, techniques and systems available for effective goal setting. It is not my intention here to duplicate these efforts. However, the systems, techniques and sets of instructions are irrelevant if you are so preoccupied with the inconsequential that you have no goals to set. No plan of life would be complete without a vision of the shore, a look at the destination. The artist must see the finished painting in order to create. The architect must see the finished building. Where we look determines where we will end up. If we run to and fro, taking pictures with a camera that is out of focus, we will get nothing but blurry pictures in return. This is precisely where we are in America today. Our camera is out of focus and everything we produce seems to be ill-defined and imperfect. Not setting goals will also result in returns in life that are out of focus and not in line with what we might have received for our efforts. This is often more a matter of elimination than inclusion. What I mean by this is, if I decide I want to be well-read it is not a function of going to the local library and starting at the first stack and reading my way through the entire library. First of all, this would preclude setting goals in any of the other important areas of my life. In order to accomplish this task, I would probably have to devote my entire life to its conclusion. Moreover, the result I would achieve would not be becoming well-read but only reading a lot. Deciding what to read that would enable me to become well-read at the exclusion of the superfluous is a better plan.

The simple act of establishing goals is empowering. Setting goals, mentally, physically and spiritually bring a magical and mystical element to life. I hope my fundamentalist friends are not put off by the words magical or mystical. I am simply referring to the energizing, vibrant, challenging, faith giving attitudes of effective goal setting. Goal setting enables us to build a life instead of just make a living. If you and I do not take charge of our situation, our situation takes charge of us. Goal setting enables us to focus.

Some years ago, when the great swimmer, Florence Chadwick was attempting to swim the English Channel, she found herself in very bad weather where it was difficult to see her trace boat. Ms. Chadwick struggled against a goal that she would one day master. In this instance, however, enshrouded in fog and rain and high seas, just a few hundred meters from the shore, she quit. Suppose that she had been able to see her objective. Even though her lungs were bursting and her heart was pounding and fear was manifesting itself, if she had only been able to see the shore, to focus on her objective, in all probability she could have completed her journey. Obstacles are those things we see in life when we lose sight of our goals. These obstacles become larger or smaller depending on how large or small we have become. In 1920, the Mallory Expedition was once more defeated on the slopes of the Himalayas. That great peak "Everest" stood as a monumental reminder to that failure. Sir Edmund Hillery was invited to speak at the Explorer's Club in London. When he was being introduced, a curtain was drawn back to reveal a huge and panoramic view of Mt. Everest stretching from floor to ceiling and wall to wall. Sir Edmund Hillery stood before the lectern viewing his nemesis that had taken the lives of members of his team and shaking with emotion he raised his fist in defiance and proclaimed, "You can't get any bigger, but I can!" With that a great roar went up from the audience as they leapt to their feet in approval. The human heart soars in the quest of great goals.

Still, it is true that when we don't know where the finish line is, when we can't get a clear picture of what it is we are trying to achieve, sometimes our will to go on falters. As I wrote about in *The Memorial*, Crown Books, 1989, one of the great tragedies of the war in Vietnam was that America appeared to be in a time of parenthesis with no history and no future. Specific goals for that action were lost in a sea of poor leadership and indecision. Like a giant committee whose only reason for being was to foster its own existence, the war lumbered on until it finally collapsed under its own weight, confusing motion with direction and activity with results. Compare that with America's most recent involvement in the Persian Gulf. Without addressing the political vs. the military objectives, the goal was to get Saddam Hussein out of Kuwait. Highly effective leadership demonstrated in strategic planning and tactical application with a clear cut picture of the desired results achieved the goal. No aimless wandering here and no out of focus results. In the microcosm, life is exactly the same.

To be effective, goals must be personal. That means that we must focus on what we want, not what someone else wants for us. Gravitate toward what you like and are good at. Real goals and desires are God-given and inspired. When goals are right for us they never take us down a path for which we have no aptitude. Well meaning friends and relatives might suggest what they think is right for us. But if we don't have the aptitude to become a brain surgeon all of the positive thinking and effort in the world will only result in lost time and frustration. Goals must be stated positively and be realistic. This means that we should set goals that recognize the point at which we are beginning and then build from there. Wanting to be a millionaire tomorrow or a great musician or a painter or a lawyer or whatever it is you are dreaming has no basis in reality if we do not recognize the place from which we are starting. Because of this, goals should be written and specific. This does not mean that they are etched in granite. It does mean that they are pencil or ink and paper and can be evaluated, modified and reset if need be. But they must be written. Through the years, I have observed many people who return to seminar after seminar asking the same questions as before. I often ask them to show me their written goals and receive a litany of excuses. Many times, it is not new knowledge that we need but simply applying what we already know that makes the difference. This of course is what we are discussing. Mastery of fundamentals. A return to the basics. Not new knowledge but focusing on what we already know, or at least, in America as Americans, what we once knew. But, for some reason we can't seem to get the directions right. It is either that, or the directions themselves are too overwhelming, complicated, confusing or wrong. A young mother walked out on her back porch observing her little boy and two of his playmates in the process of playing with three little baby skunks, fearing the obvious, she became excited and shouted for her little boy and his friends to run away. Hearing the anxiety in her voice, they each picked up a little skunk and ran away as fast as they could. I wonder how many times you and I, not understanding the directions, much less the objective, pick up our skunks and run away still embracing the source of our problem.

The benefits of goal setting are obvious. Setting goals improves our self image. The very act of mentally considering new vistas, dreams and desires opens up greater hope for the future. Each step we take along this developmental path adds a new dimension to our life. Each small goal we achieve helps us to become more aware of our potential and builds confidence. If our values are good, our goals will be worthwhile. We begin to realize that it is not necessarily the things we achieve by goal setting that is important but rather what we become in the process. Goal setting helps us to identify our strengths and our weaknesses and provides us with a track upon which to run. The process of pursuing goals enables us to sift through their importance, and, like the business person we discussed earlier taking inventory at the end of each year, we may decide that continuing to commit time, energy and money to a particular strategy is no longer worthwhile. While this may seem to fly in the face of Winston Churchill and the "never quit" syndrome and irritate some of the positive thinkers, I would remind them of *Proverbs 13:19*, "It is pleasant to see plans develop. That is why fools refuse to give them up even when they are wrong." Goal setting enables us to separate reality from wishful thinking. Finally, if these benefits were not enough, goal setting can extend our lives. It has long been recognized that people who retire to something, that is, are able to divert their energies to new goals in life live nine times longer than their counterparts who rock their lives away on the front porch of old folks Florida.

Why is it then, if goal setting is so obviously useful, that more people do not participate in a positive manner? I do not believe that lack of knowledge is the answer. Most people today have at least a rudimentary understanding of how to set goals. The more important question is, why don't they? Implicit in goal setting is change. Change often involves a period of chaos. Many people, even those whose lives are in pain and discomfort, prefer the predictability of unhappiness rather than the unpredictability of change. Their self talk betrays this attitude. They often will say things like, its really not important that I lose this weight or get that promotion or write that book. They try to convince themselves and others that the results really don't make any difference to them. Do you remember in Lewis Carroll's "Alice in Wonderland" when Alice met the Cheshire Cat at the crossroads what happened? "Cheshire-Puss," ... said Alice, "would you tell me, please, which way I ought to go from here?" "That depends a good deal on where you want to get to," said the Cat. "I don't much care where–" said Alice. "Then it doesn't matter which way you go" said the Cat. –" so long as I get somewhere," Alice added as an explanation. "Oh you're sure to do that." said the Cat, "if you only walk long enough." And so it is for us. And so it is for America. George Bush lost the presidency to Bill Clinton, largely because he could not define a great mission for our country. People even talked about the "vision thing" as a weakness. If we have not examined our values, priorities and purposes, and if, as a result we do not have any clearly defined goals, then the path we choose to take really doesn't make any difference. Instead, life becomes a survival course. Preoccupied with the inconsequential, rolled in doubt, wrapped in unbelief, believing the biggest lies of the uncommitted, we fail to embrace the simplest truths. So, here we are living at a time when people no longer agree on the rules that govern behavior. With no eternal values and no goals it appears except to satisfy pleasures, traditional restraints on behavior collapses. Without goals victimism reigns and parasitism is born. Sucking off the public teat becomes a right instead of a privilege and institutionalized corruption begets a government that runs up a 4 trillion dollar debt. With lack of focus and lack of quality goals the drug of the Great Society becomes food stamps and welfare. As Dodo said after the race in *Alice in Wonderland*, "Everybody has won and we all must have prizes."

Once a very old man, barely able to walk, brought a painting to the great master painter of his time. With gnarled hands he lovingly presented the master with his offering. The master, taken aback with the beauty and depth of the work, became very excited. Who painted this he cried, his plaintive voice more of a demand than a request. The old man, weary with age, looked into the face of the great master and replied, "A twelve year old boy." No! the master retorted. Bring him to me and I will make him a great artist, famous and world renown. The old man, shaking with emotion and tears in his eyes, looking into the face of the master replied, "Alas, I cannot, for I was that youth." A young boy is a theory. An old man is a fact. We must return to goals in which democracy can flourish. Hard work, responsibility, goals that cause our young people to reach outside themselves in inspiration and concern for community and country.

With or without goals, you and I will spend twenty years of our lives sleeping, three years waiting on others, one year on the telephone, four months tying our shoes and six years watching television. Like Alice, most of us have a desire to go somewhere. Interestingly enough, we are always on the way. This is the quest and the journey. It is a process of becoming. Since all of our life is controlled by our goals, whether we chose to consciously set them or not, deciding what kind of goals we will set is the first step toward living life with value and purpose. And, while there are great chunks of life which can be both routine and monotonous, if we do nothing that is important to us we will ultimately conclude that we are unimportant as well. I wonder if these were not the people that Thoreau was reflecting upon when he said most of us live lives of quiet desperation.

If the statistics are true that only 3% of all people effectively set goals and that those 3% do far more with their lives than the 97% that do not, then that quiet desperation must be the frustration that comes from being at sea, goal-less, out of control and without hope. Clearly, this is a simple fundamental. Simple to grasp but apparently not so simple to apply. I will leave the art of goal setting to the multitude of books, seminars and cassettes available for you to embrace. But I do exhort you to look out and up in hope to seek a basic purpose and a new dream. I ask you to ponder the end of the track. And later, when we focus on time and death, I will ask you to ponder the fervor, untested idealism, rejection, pain, failure and loneliness with which we often approach life. Our life's purpose is paramount, our goals empowering and significant.

One final note. All goals tarnish with time if not renewed in some way. Everyone in the business world is talking about renewal today. Reinventing companies is the catch word for those pouring over the Harvard Business Review, Sloan's Management and the Wall Street Journal. A recent edition of Business Week was dedicated to Reinventing America. They hit the nail right on the head. In the world of international business in recent years, we were bludgeoned by the Japanese and the Germans. As a country, we then embraced the mentality of a victim and cried "foul" to our international competitors when the truth is we simply got our socks knocked off by people who were more focused than we were, who defined their goals and pursued them with passion. And, what's more, while we demanded our rights as laborers and workers, they were willing to do what we once were...whatever it takes.

Frankly, they did it with process and systems that we created. Take Japan, for example. We exported systems and process and W. E. Deming became a legend. Years later, they exported the very things we gave them back to us and called them quality circles, JIT, and Z management. We embraced these "new ideas" wholeheartedly and failed in their application because we forgot the soft issues of business that were already mandated in their culture when we gave them the hard issues. More recently, Japan and other "Asian Tigers" have been suffering because they forgot the values that are the fundamental support for both the hard and soft issues. We will be examining these values in the next fundamental. Nonetheless, these soft issues are exactly what we have been talking about. Goals that are meaningful to people that drive the process of business. Goals that are meaningful to people that drive America. Goals that give people self-respect, purpose, honor, dignity and a reason to expend discretionary energy on their own because they believe in the dream.

This process of becoming then is not one of endings but of beginnings. Success is the progressive realization of a worthwhile dream and planning and goal setting is the best kind of dreaming because it enables us to imagine what the future could be like. We need to dream great dreams. This is the stuff of which life is made. We need to imagine what could be and say, why not? Don't wait for that moment of truth to force you into evaluating your priorities and goals. The accident, the death, the tragedy, the wife or husband that walks out, the crisis that causes us to begin the journey inward. Paraphrasing General Douglas MacArthur, people do not grow old by years, they grow old by deserting their ideals and dreams. Tears may wrinkle the skin but giving up on our dreams and goals wrinkle the soul. Dream the great dreams. Set goals that stretch. Believe. Become a master goal setter. **Focus on the goal.**

RECOMMENDED READING:

Success The Glenn Bland Method: Bland

Success Motivation and The Scriptures: Cook

How To Reach Your Life's Goals: Daniel

We have staked the whole future of American civilization, not upon the power of government, far from it.

We have staked the future of all of our political institutions upon the capacity of mankind for self-government; ourselves, to sustain ourselves according to the Ten Commandments of God.

- James Madison

History fails to record a single precedent in which nations subject to moral decay have not passed into political and economic decline.

There has been either a spiritual awakening to overcome the moral lapse or a progressive deterioration leading to ultimate national disaster.

- Gen. Douglas MacArthur

V

FOCUS ON: VALUES

In Alan Bloom's book, *The Closing of The American Mind*, he reflects on how looking into the faces of his freshman classes he knows they believe only two things. One, that truth is a matter of opinion and two, that all morality is a matter of preference. While a possible overstatement, there is little difficulty within our culture of finding ample evidence to support such a thesis. With no absolute foundation for truth or morality what we seem to have embraced is a value system that has resulted in confusion and, as can be seen in examples such as the LA riots, anarchy. When God is removed from reality, chaos is inevitable and the result is a "man" centered philosophy that ends with a steady decline in values.

Values are the foundation of all order and these are inherent in human nature. As stated in the prologue, we are born with a sense of what is right and wrong. Telling the truth as opposed to lying, not stealing, not killing, honoring another's property are all inherent matters of conscience. Conscience, incidentally, connects us with the highest that we know or hold in most reverence. Conscience tells me what the highest I know demands I do. It is the eye of the soul that looks up toward God or out toward what we hold as the highest. Therefore, conscience motivates people in different ways. Perhaps we should ask ourselves, do I value what God values and love what God loves? Do I value highly the things that please God? Are my affections and goals fixed on eternal values? These values are part of humanness but can be obviated by neglect and denial, rejection, poor example, lack of education and reinforcement. Values are the bedrock of our democratic system. They are imbedded in the hearts and spirits of our founding fathers. In fact, Jefferson referred to them as "ancient principles" and it was upon these principles that our national goals of freedom, prosperity and peace would rest. Principles are eternal. "They stem not from our resolution or lack of it but from elsewhere, where in patient and infinite ranks they simply want to be called."[7]

However, what our public schools teach today is values clarification that imputes that there are no eternal truths. The book of Judges refers to this when it says, "Everyone did that which was right in his own eyes." So, we have replaced the Bible in school with muggings, robberies, rapes and murders. The ancient principles that Jefferson referred to that were to be the rock foundation for freedom, prosperity and peace have been replaced by the brittle clay of secularism floating in a sea of moral decay.

In focusing on the dream, I quoted *Proverbs 29:18* to point out that where there is no vision the people perish. But it also says "where there is no dream the people cast off restraint." What this means is that there is a big difference between an ideal and a dream. The true dream imparts moral incentive if it is God authored. However, when we lose sight of God, restraints are cast off. There is no prayer. There is no moral baseline in which to judge action taken. We become reckless, acting on our own initiative, bearing the brunt of a self-centered lifestyle that comes back on individuals as well as nations. God is dethroned and man is deified. Human reason reigns supreme. I believe that we are at the crossroads. Thomas Jefferson once said, "Indeed, I tremble for my country when I reflect that God is just and that His justice cannot sleep forever." Can the liberties of a nation be thought secure, when we have removed their only firm basis, a conviction in the minds of people that these liberties are the gift of God.

The heart and soul of any balanced organization or country is a set of core operating values. If the dream provides the impetus, values declare the boundary for behavior. You simply can't build anything, not even an outhouse, to last without a solid foundation. The dream and values are inextricably bound together. Values provide the moral courage when things get tough in pursuit of the dream. They create an atmosphere of common purpose and truth and help us to set priorities.

Before I went to Vietnam for the first time, the Marine Corp had created a Viet Cong village in the woods at Quantico, VA. For about a month, as I recall, as part of mastering fundamentals, we did reaction drills entering that village from many different places and times, to test reaction and readiness. I am certain these reaction drills saved my life more than once in Vietnam. Those oft repeated drills were just like values that become anchors in the storm - telling us what to do and where to go. They settle our future, and when drawn on hastily, they cut to the core, setting boundaries for our actions and defining who we really are. While there is no hope without the dream, without values we are awash in a sea of indecision. Since we are what we habitually think and do, without values we can only look out for number one, as reflected in all of the literature recently spawned that encourages us to focus on I, me and power. Values meet us head on at the moments of truth in life that determine success or failure.

Oliver Wendell Holmes, Jr. said, "Historic continuity with the past is not a duty it is a necessity." But what have we done? We have taken great delight in ripping apart historical values and anchors, as well as leaders from the past.

We have taught our children upside down and backward- allowing losers to tell people how to win. No amount of traveling down the wrong road will take us to the right destination. God help us for not telling the young people who they are. God help us for not articulating the dream. God help us for not setting the boundaries and instilling faith by telling them why they would work. Values have simply not been taught. Not in church, home, school or by example. Instead, we now ask our children to return to a value based society that has not existed in their lifetime. Or, perhaps the truth is that there never were traditional values but only people who aspired to them in intermittent sin. Now, we appear to have lost sight of even the aspirations, our collective conscience revering things far below God.

Writing in the February 1992 issue of *Time Magazine*, Robert Hughes said,"there must be values in the home based on the Word of God." Everyone is living with some set of values. Man's chief purpose is to establish and preserve values. Values are not, as Bertrand Russell once suggested, a matter of taste and perception. Values are instead exact and understandable. They are clear statements of policy upon which a business, home, organization, church or country are established and built. Do we need to point out such values? Maybe we do.

Authority is a value that is based on God ordained leadership. Obedience is a value that has its foundation in character. We cannot save ourselves or sanctify ourselves, only God can do that. God will not give us good habits nor will He give us character. That is up to us and it requires adopting the right habits that should become just as rote as the reaction drills we did before going to Vietnam. When decisions are required or crisis comes, we need to know what to do by applying the right habit based on foundational values. Work ethic is another value that should be applied on the job, in the home or as a father or mother. What about courtesy, dedication, determination or money and its use so that it can be used wisely and given generously. How about sanctity of life. The glory of life comes from what we revere and hold dear. Yet, through abortion, infanticide and euthanasia we threaten life and argue murder as if it were a point of legality instead of a value paradigm shift in our society.

Rousseau said that reason deceives us, but conscience never will. But what if our intellectual conscience only reflects the lowest that we know. And how does that stand up against a recent Associated Press article that Houston teenagers are three times more liable to be wounded or shot to death than the average student and that they are also doing most of the shooting. In explaining it, Lt. Greg Neely said,

"They don't have a conscience because they have not been taught to have a conscience...they have no remorse because they don't value life. "[8] Senator Robert Byrd recently stated in roll call, "On most given nights, with a flick of a remote-control device the living rooms of average American families can be treated to a melange of foul-mouthed brats uttering language for which any stranger entering those same living rooms and uttering that same language would probably be thrown out bodily and the use of which in any polite company would earn its user a reputation as a boor and a lout."[9] Marion Wright Edelman, the founder of Children's Defense Fund, recently said, "Parenting...nurturing the next generation, is the most important function of this society, and we've got to take it seriously." She says, "We must place our kids first in both our private actions and our public actions...We talk about family values, but when we look at our policies, we don't do it."[10] At the commencement address for Notre Dame University in South Bend Indiana, then President George Bush said that "America will remain at risk unless it reverses the breakdown of the family." He called Americans to support Pope John Paul II's appeal for "a new social climate of moral accountability in which to raise our children." Mr. Bush further stated that parents must teach their children the dignity of work and instill a work ethic in the kids.[11] Interestingly enough, Bill Murchison tells of a discussion he had recently with the senior superintendent of the Moscow Public Education Department, a deputy minister of education and the Moscow city councilman responsible for education. They were telling why religion has been introduced into the public schools of communism's former world capital. Here is why: The ex-Soviet Union's moral wreckage may eclipse in size and weight its economic wreckage. "There are no values in our society" said the Moscow councilman, one Valentin Yefremov. This, after 74 years of orders to venerate the Communist Party. "The biggest question for education is the moral education of young people," said the deputy minister, one Dr. Lubov Kezina. This, after relentless attempts by communist educators to demonstrate that bourgeois morality was a snare and a delusion. Murchison goes on to say that the great teaching institutions of any society are family, church and schools but that for the past 20 or 30 years American schools have trafficked in moral neutrality. He suggests that a mention on public premises that a traditional morality is right would likely bring vigilantes swooping down declaring separation of church and state, or the like. Bluntly, the children are not safe in classroom, cafeteria or hallway because the schools have become microcosms of the larger society. What is going on here?[12] In his book *The Devaluing of America*, former U. S. Education Secretary Bill Bennett makes the case for moral instruction saying honesty, fairness, self-discipline, fidelity to task, friends and family, personal responsibility[13] are at the crux of the matter.

But what about our new morality or petty morality as Walter Williams calls it. We give condoms and birth control devices to our children. Teen music preaches sex, racism and violence. Welfare programs subsidize immoral behavior. Social misfits and social parasites have become society's mascots. Wasting and expending the gifts of previous generations, politicians are seen as sensitive and applauded for taking the property of one American and giving it to another, turning their failures into success. Criminals who commit despicable acts are labeled sick and hence just like a person who has the flu, can hardly be blamed. As we have seen with Bill Clinton and Monica Lewinsky, having a president who's engaged in a bit of extramarital hanky-panky appears far less destructive to our new values and moral standards. Unless there's a moral rejuvenation in America, we're going to continue our national decline.[14] We must focus on fundamentals. At the heart of the commitment to excellence is a constant emphasis on fundamentals. Returning to the basics, those values rooted in a conscience that reveres the highest, truly settles our future. First as individuals and then collectively as a nation. The fundamental of values, like all the others, is part of the journey. Not purchased or grasped or yanked out of life, values are earned. I could not describe it better than Kristin Leffel, Grade 7, from Sequoyah Middle School in Edmond, Oklahoma. Kristen was a winner in the young writers contest foundation when she wrote the following:

THE VALUE STORE OF LIFE

What could I buy in a value store? What would it contain? Would I have enough money? As I walked into the store, I looked over my shopping list. The list read: religious faith, family life, friendship, happiness, and financial success.

The first item on my list was religious faith. I strolled down the aisles until I came to it. The price tag read $400. It is very expensive but very important in my life. This value is worth more than money can buy; therefore I am willing to purchase this value at the bargain price of $400, and into my value basket I placed it.

The second item on my list was family life. When I came upon family life, the price tag read "sale," $250. Family life is important and worth far more than the $250 price. I could not pass up this bargain, so I placed it in my value basket along with my religious faith.

As I walked further down the aisle, I came upon friendship. The price for friendship was $175. I thought to myself that friendship was pretty cheap. Many people would die for friendship, it is such a precious value. I looked over all the friendships, picked out one that I felt was very special, and placed it in my value basket along with religious faith and family life.

The next thing on my list was happiness. When I came upon happiness, I searched for a price tag. When I found it I first could not make out the price, but finally I determined that it was $100, fifty percent of the original price. It was on sale. Some people spend thousands of dollars on happiness and I only had to pay $100. I wondered how something so valuable could be so cheap. I held happiness very tightly and gently set it in my value basket.

Finally I was on the last item on my list which read financial success. This item was easy to find. The price on it read $75. Was this really a bargain? To some people this item would be very expensive, but to me it was not even worth $75. Ashamed, I put it down into my value basket.

When the clerk rang up all the items, the total came to $1000. He said that he did not know why people bought values when they could earn them. He asked me in a low voice, "Isn't that what life is about?" As I walked out of the store, I felt ashamed. The clerk was right. You do not buy values, you earn them.[15]

We cannot pay cash for values anymore than, as the comedian, Father Guido Sarducci recommends, we can pay cash for our sins at $.25 a pop. We simply reap what we sow. C. S. Lewis wrote, "We laugh at honor and are surprised to find traitors in our midst." What is so amazing is as Emerson said, "Society is always taken by surprise at any new example of common sense." How can we thumb our noses at moral duty to others and our country? How can we fail our children in giving them the character gifts our parents gave us, self respect, independence, honesty, thrift, respect for others? Walter Williams said it this way, "Today's Americans truly deserve the national decline and calamity that await us, but future generations don't. National immorality has led to a squandering of the resources bequeathed us by our forebears. We have come to believe that Congress should use extortion to make it possible for one person to live at another's expense. This idea is turning us into a nation of thieves where we believe, for example, "If Congress rips me off for the benefit of farmers and savings and loans, I ought to be able to rip off somebody else for my benefit."

Most problems we face today result from a systemic decline in national morality. It starts from the way we raise children and continues through adulthood, where thrift is a vice and debt a virtue. Then, in our late years, we use Social Security to live off our children and saddle our grandchildren with inescapable debt. Will we regain our morality, or will we continue to imitate other once-great nations of the past?[16]

A lack of values and spiritual tempering leads to evil without restraint. About five years ago, at one of our business locations, four young girls were found shot to death. Hands tied, a bullet in the back of their heads and then burned by people with no soul. Beautiful young ladies, modeling one set of values taught by their parents of dignity and diligence and hard work, defiled and taken from us by a member of a society bereft of values built on a foundation of sand. The Chief of Police later commented, "Do you want to know fear? Just wait until this generation of young people become adults. Most have no conscience, they have no soul, they kill and wonder why we are even concerned."

When we focus on the fundamental of choice we will see that there are thousands of day to day decisions about values. Each time we make one of these decisions we must evaluate ourselves and then follow that choice. Every time I have had the opportunity to instill moral values into a business entity in the corporate world the results were astounding. When values and beliefs become embodied in the work place they intensify employees commitment, enthusiasm and drive. Once they are embedded in the warp and woof of a business, communication improves. Values lift the integrity of management's decision making and a manager's ability to evaluate personnel and projects. One of the first things I did after taking over the helm of Mail Boxes Etc. was to bring in Sister Suzanne Donovan, a catholic nun, to lead our entire company in determining these values. I have worked with Suzanne for about 10 years now in strategic and annual operating planning. Every associate, board member, selected members of our franchise family and vendor community participated. The values they developed over a week's time were caring, honesty, fairness, integrity, trust, respect, commitment and accountability. It is my opinion that in today's business world you should be willing to experiment with and change anything at any time with the single exception of values....they are inviolate. And, as it is for business, so it is for our country. Defending values requires constant vigilance and is one of those responsibilities along with being the organizational symbol and clarifying the vision that a leader cannot delegate.

Just as it did for the individuals that took the lives of those young ladies, choices make up a portrait of who we are. And, in a larger venue, the collective choices we make become a portrait of America. Larger life issues are always determined by small scale choices. We must be anchored in the right message. We must focus on core values such as those recommended by Linda and Richard Eyres in their book "Teaching Values to Children". Honesty, courage, peaceability, self-reliance and potential, self-discipline and moderation, fidelity and charity, loyalty and dependability, respect, love, unselfishness and sensitivity, kindness and friendliness, justice and mercy.

The structural integrity of our lives and our country depends on the center around which we integrate our lives. As the Eyres point out, we must teach moral values to our children because it is the only way they will know happiness or find the truth. We have eliminated God from our classroom and we are in danger of eliminating ourselves. We need truth. We need to stand up for what is right. We must win America back one heart at a time. **Focus on values.**

RECOMMENDED READING:

Living Without Losing: Don Polston

Man's Search for Meaning: Viktor Frankl

Road Less Traveled: Scott Peck

America lives in the heart of every man everywhere
who wishes to find a region
where he will be free to
work out his destiny as he chooses.

- Woodrow Wilson

The choices you make in moral and religious questions
determine the way America will go.

The choice before us is plain, Christ or chaos,
conviction or compromise, discipline and disintegration.

I am rather tired about hearing about our
rights and privileges as American citizens.

The time has come, it is now, when we ought
to hear about the duties and responsibilities of our
citizenship.

America's future depends upon her accepting
and demonstrating God's government.

It is just as plain and clear as that.

- Peter Marshall

VI

FOCUS ON: CHOICE

To live life is to choose. God made us as beings capable of choosing. All life is a choice and the choices you make determine the life you lead. You choose everything you do. You run your own life and there are no limitations on your power to choose, except one. You and I cannot make choices for anyone else but ourselves. We do decide not to let ourselves know we are choosing from time to time but the only limits in the power of choice are limits of belief. In fact, what has become of America and the human race, in general, is a result of choices made of our own free will.

We are responsible for our lives and once we accept the responsibility of choice in our lives new revelations spring from old truths. Pain, confusion, difficulty, unhappiness, lying are all choices. We may lie to buffer ourselves from the unhappiness of other wrong choices or to keep from feeling stupid or foolish but lying itself is a choice that compounds the original choice, blocking self-insight and interpersonal contact. Truth, on the other hand, opens up communications and enables us to grow. Like lying, it is also a choice.

Every situation begs a response. Hope or fear, encouragement or criticism, belief or despair, we largely get what we choose. Life is a matter of choice and expectation. Fear destroys our confidence and worry our will to go on. Jealousy destroys relationships and an unwillingness to forgive ultimately destroys ourselves. So, why not make a different choice? Through arrogance, willfulness and conceit we have earned our punishment. It's not just who we are but the choices we make with what we have been given that makes the difference.

The negative or pessimistic side of choosing often leads to addiction, both physical and emotional. The German word for worry, as an example, is wurgen, which means to choke. Worry can become so much a matter of choice that it is addictive. It is also contagious and often leaves a wake of destruction in its path that stretches a lifetime. This is why the structural integrity of our lives depends on the center or the core around which we make our choices. We must be anchored in the right message.

Examining our values as we already discussed, is crucial. These fundamental values drive the choices we make. The thousands of day-to-day decisions we make require us to follow our choices and ultimately create a picture of who we really are. The larger issues of our lives, over time, are decided by these small choices we make every day. As individuals, as people, as a country and a world, we are either made greater or denigrated by these small choices. Contrary to our casual scoffing of decisions we made twenty years ago, choices, even youthful choices, are important. They generate effects throughout life. A person who cannot manage personal passions as a matter of course cannot manage others. How often have we seen a promising beginning followed by a bad choice that leads to a tragic ending?

After years of manipulation and deceit, morality and traditional values are no longer posh or in vogue. What we end up with is an entire menu of value systems from which we can choose. We must ask ourselves who is teaching who. We must be anchored in the right message or we become sitting ducks for bad choices. Regardless of the victim mindset that permeates our society today, we are not innocent. Yes, we are victims but we are victims of our own bad choices.

The wind and the rain or storms of life do not determine our destiny. Neither do other people and their opinions determine our future. What does affect our lives is our power to choose. We can:

choose to do something good

choose to have a good attitude

choose to make people an asset

choose to make enemies friends

choose to laugh

choose to be responsible for our actions

choose to give and serve

We have seen how important it is to focus on dreams and goals. But the full measure of life is measured not by the objectives we achieve but by who and what we are becoming in their pursuit. What we do to achieve these goals are the choices we make everyday. Nothing happens until you want it to happen, for the greatest goals are achieved in the heart, not the head. When my daughters were small, my wife and I took them to see Sandy Duncan in "Peter Pan." Ms. Duncan sang a song that I have never forgotten about how to find "never never land." She sang that this magic place would not be located on a map or chart but that the only way you could find it was in your heart. This is where the great dreams and goals and choices lie...in the heart. For it is out of the abundance of the heart that the mouth speaks and choices are made.

But with great dreams, come great challenges and problems. How we choose to react to those problems determine our destiny and develops our character, both as an individual and as a country. There is always a way out and a choice. As Longfellow said, "The lowest ebb is the turn of the tide." Choose to view the battlefield from the victor's side. Choose to know that things will get better, that God answers prayer. Choose to have faith and add a dimension to life that defies all logical explanation. Niel Eskelein in his book *Yes Yes Living in a No No World* said,

I choose to serve one God

I choose to worship Him in spirit and truth

I choose to praise His name

I choose to keep His day sacred

I choose to respect my parents

I choose to respect and preserve life

I choose to be faithful in marriage

I choose to work for what I need

I choose to tell the truth

I choose to be content with what I have

I choose to greet this day with love in my heart

Time and time again, in business and personal life, I am reinforced that we get what we choose to expect. I cannot tell you how many times in the last twenty-five years I have seen men and women choose their own destiny. Whether in the fox holes of Vietnam or the corporate halls of America, the choices to win or lose, to look up or look down, to be grateful or prideful have been made every day. You must choose to believe. Thinking does not produce hope nor logic faith. These are choices. Choosing to expect the best in life is a dynamic force. This is where we really live, it is the real us. There are simply no hopeless situations, only people who choose to be hopeless. Choose to invest in yourself by making the right choices. People constantly ask me how I find time to write with an extraordinary business schedule. The answer, of course, is the same for watching television. You have to invest the time.

For example, *The Memorial* took me nearly six years to complete. The work you are reading took nearly an equal amount of time.

In Christopher Columbus' diary he wrote, "This day we sailed on." Hunger, sickness, storm, whatever – "This day we sailed on." That is a choice. Don't get lost in living between the failures of yesterday and the fears of tomorrow. Choose something else. Choose to:

like people

dream big dreams

speak the truth

not accept failure

live in faith

live an exciting life

show mercy

show love

embrace a positive attitude

rejoice

be a helper

do good

be patient

love God

have faith in God

believe God

obey God

It is amazing to me that this concept of selection or choice is scoffed at by so many people. Particularly today with the victim mentality so pervasive in our society, perpetuated by a cadre of attorneys and self-help parasites who obviate all personal responsibility for the sake of a buck. Yet, people who worry simply practice positive thinking in reverse. Choosing the problem or choosing evil is an end in itself. Petty, vindictive, mean-spirited, angry, we often sacrifice principle for pleasure while losing the abstract concepts of loyalty, integrity, sincerity and forgiveness or blow them off with astonishing speed while choosing to be unaware that we are doing so.

Everything in life is under our power of choice, but once the choice is made, we become the servant to the choice.

The choice of drug use makes a slave of substance abusers; dropping out of school produces poverty, paupers indentured to ignorance and the limitations it brings; our choice of a marriage partner can make marriage become a rich, rewarding life or a poor existence. Selecting the right food and opting for exercise will serve the body well so it can be worn in good health. Enjoying the disciplines of study and developing the powers of concentration serve knowledge which translates into authority, submission to patience is the key to finding the right woman.

CHOICES DETERMINE DESTINY.[17]

In the recent Presidential elections, it has amazed me that so many people, particularly Christians, chose to cast votes for candidates that appeared to embrace lying, adultery, abortion and cowardice for the sake of expediency. It seems we have progressed from self-denial to an assumption of self-goodness to a capacity to project that same assumption of innate goodness and innocence to others when it meets our purpose. We know we are guilty but we deny it. A former Mayor of Washington, D. C. can be caught in adultery and filmed smoking cocaine and yet, in a cloud of self-offending protestation of innocence, be re-elected. We have seen politicians and businessmen and women and pastors openly lie and then climb a mountain of self-delusion for years to keep others from finding out they are not what they appear. These are choices.

Mr. Josephson, founder of the Los Angeles Institute for the Advancement of Ethics, which promotes ethical behavior, disclosed the results of a two-year study on ethics at a meeting of the commonwealth Club of California.

Among the study's findings:

33 percent of high school students surveyed and 16 percent of college students admitted that they had stolen something from a store within the past year.

Sixty-one percent of the high school students and 32 percent of college students admitted that they cheated on an exam in the past year.

More than one-third of all high school and college students said they would lie on a resume or job application to get a job.

Twenty-one percent of college students said they would falsify a report if it was necessary to keep their job.

In Dostoveski's *The Brothers Karamazov*, Ivan, an atheist, tells his believing brother Alonzorba a story about a ninety year old Cardinal called the Grand Inquisitor. The Grand Inquisitor challenges Christ in his return to earth. He is furious at Christ for giving man the power to choose. We are not intelligent enough, we are not moral enough, we are not courageous enough to have such awesome power. Of Christ's choice to take the bread of heaven and not the devil's offering in the wilderness, he literally rebukes Jesus saying, "Thou wouldst not deprive man of freedom, thinking what is freedom worth if it is bought with bread?" He concludes that it is far too much to weigh down humanity with...the fearful burden of choice.

To choose is a fearful burden as Ivan said but it is also a great gift. Even that is a choice. We cannot overcome our limitations by ourselves. The human record is moved from start to finish with evil. We are cruel, exploitive, lustful, vengeful and unforgiving. We are all wounded. We are all flawed. Not one of us is free from the potential of SIN regardless of its form. In the OLD TESTAMENT book of Jeremiah we are told that the heart is deceitful above all else and we remain a mystery, even to ourselves.

Yet, we continue to listen to the wrong voices. We are taught upside down and backwards by losers telling us how to win. Adam and Eve made the wrong choice by listening to an animal that was created lower than they were. You and I have been doing the same thing ever since. We live in a moral universe and the problem with humanity is moral. Every choice has a consequence. Just as the momentous choice Adam and Eve made had external consequences, so do the evil choices we make grow. Choices that appear of no import, so small, so inconsequential, leave us bewildered at the enormity of the consequences. For Good or Evil it makes no difference. From one idea in the head of one man 6 million Jews were exterminated. All life pales before this stupendous power of choice. And, in the end, we are powerless to come up with a solution to fix the problem we created ourselves. In the end, it is God who triumphs. Grace over nature and mercy over justice is offered by a loving God Who chose to make us whole again by substituting Himself as payment for our wrong choices. And what should our response be? Perhaps, love, joy, peace, patience, kindness, goodness, faithfulness, gentleness, self-control. The choice is still ours. We must choose to be anchored in the right message. To stand on a firm foundation. Choose personal responsibility. Choose to deny denial.

Life is not without purpose or direction, it's just that we have been choosing to receive the wrong message far too long. We are not victims, we are victors. Evil never has the last word. God does. Choose to look up. All of the buzzwords of business will not overcome moral flabbiness. It was not the 100 year strategic plan of the Japanese that caused their recent economic downturn but making wrong choices about values and trust that led to economic destruction. All of the success ascribed to the wealthy and powerful provides them with no greater power than you and I have. For the final choice, even after death, is that we will still be what we have chosen. The choices we make in life are critical. In the final analysis, you get what you choose. Seek and ye shall find is not a Biblical promise of mercy, it is a basic truth of life that works for both good and evil. Never before has there been a time when we should be able to recognize this more than in modern America.

If you think you are undeserving or incapable of making right choices, remember, God chose to send his Son for you. Grace, forgiveness and love is now yours if you too will but choose. This is the ultimate dream and the ultimate choice.

Choose to dream big. Choose to act now, for if you do not choose to move nothing happens. That book doesn't get written, the speech prepared, the degree achieved, the project finished, the career changed, the date made, eternity embraced...nothing. Not choosing is still a choice and we get what we choose.

Sing while you can. Write while there is ink in the pen. Choose to be determined. Choose to invest in life. Choose to focus on what is left, not what you have lost. Choose to not fear poverty, failure, criticism, ill health, loss of love or old age. You have been given life and while you have breath there is hope. And, if you have made the right choice in life, even in death there is still hope. Choose to keep looking up! **Focus on choice.**

RECOMMENDED READING:

Choice: Og Mandino

Choices: Helmstelten

Choices With Clout: Cross

*Historically, the American people
have yearned mightily for leadership
and have consistently mistrusted
and maligned it whenever it appeared.*

- Samuel B. Gould

We must have many Lincoln-hearted men.

- Vachel Lindsay

VII

FOCUS ON: LEADERSHIP

MacGregor Burns in his book on leadership writes that the genius of leadership lies in the manner in which leaders see and act on their own and their follower's values and motivations.

This reflects what I call diamond vision. With first quality diamonds the clarity and color is designated by a VV rating. In leadership, the VV rating relates to values and vision. It is the values, coupled with vision, that keep an organization or a country on course. The power of leadership rests not on the individual but the purpose, vision and values they represent. When strong ethics are combined with a positive belief in others and imbued with the power of the dream or vision, there is dynamism and unity. Values, vision and unity provide the VUE (view) for servant leadership.

Like first quality diamonds, servant leaders are rare. This is because companies, organizations and political systems become metastasized with bureaucracy and self-interest. Those few with the courage to do and say what they believe is right fall by the wayside while those that remain are often ostracized, forced out or choose to leave. What remains is a compromise. Surely, our political system in America is a perfect example of this process. Situational ethics and situational management should be prone to failure in life and business but they are surviving in today's moral climate. Deception and insensitivity should not be the raw materials for leadership. What is needed is integrity and consistency. Personal beliefs and values bring a sense of rightness and moral soundness to any organization This is what diamond vision is all about. Values, vision and unity. As previously stated, areas in which a leader cannot compromise or delegate. The offshoot of diamond vision is the leadership council. Not authoritative or political, but encouraging. Desiring to do the right thing and basing everything on trust, this is the fertile ground in which servant leadership grows. Servant leadership happens when the leadership council begins to elevate each other to higher levels of motivation, morals and performance. When leadership is sought for the right motives, it becomes the most privileged work in the world. At Mail Boxes Etc., we have 10 members of the leadership council made up of the Chief Executive Officer, Chief Operating Officer, Executive Vice Presidents, & Vice Presidents. We meet every Tuesday morning at 7:30 am in closed session where the "shoulder boards" come off and we cross pollinate all disciplines. Each Vice President understands that they are there to serve all members of our MBE family, including US Office Products, our parent company, each associate, franchisee and shareholder. Our entire existence is focused customer intimacy in that we must know and meet the needs of our MBE family.

Within that environment, they are free to make any decision independently except those that might drill a hole below the water line. All of those decisions come before the council. Where consensus is not reached, I reserve a "Primus Inter Pares" right of "first amongst equals" to break the deadlock.

What makes the difference today is the leadership. People have to be led by one who inspires confidence. They will follow a leader who shows him or herself wise and has the courage to stand on what they believe. In this sense, leadership is not elected or appointed it is earned. Unlike so many of our would-be leaders today, the transformational leader knows where he stands. As I write this, I listen to the controversy over national leaders and their apparent inability to define what they believe, inspire people to follow and take them there. A leader simply cannot be neutral morally and spiritually and maintain integrity and wisdom.

Cal Thomas pointed out in *Viewpoints*, "We need leaders who will confront our moral decay and call people to virtue, even at the risk of being labeled leftover Puritans. We need leaders to say divorce and one-parent families are not alternative lifestyles but forms of adult behavior with profoundly destructive consequences for children.

We need leaders with the courage to say that more government spending does not mean more compassion - and that policies and programs cannot touch hearts that require change.

We need leaders who will encourage us to sacrifice for our children and love our spouses, even when love is difficult - in spite of the consequences, in spite of the spirit of our age.

Our failure of courage is not only in politics. It pervades our society. It does little good to blame government when the voice of these values is equally weak almost everywhere else. Perhaps instead of constantly searching for new leaders, we need to be new leaders - in our families and communities."[18]

Power never has made America great. Goodness and virtue have. If we lose these fundamental commodities, no missiles and no economy can defend us from destruction.

As we are seeing an unprecedented fashion in today's world, and as we have seen throughout history, failures in leadership cannot or should not be tolerated long. There are very few leaders among the many managers and supervisors in business today. In time, effective new leaders must be found. The one characteristic common to all leaders is the capacity to make things happen. While the leader is often a good manager, the good manager may not be a good leader because leaders are able to motivate people to action. Leaders anywhere have strong egos and forceful personalities. But no one is a born leader. Egos and personalities will run rampant without boundaries. Visible examples of such leaders were Hitler, Stalin, and more recently Saddam Hussein and David Koresh. Not many who aspire to leadership are willing to pay the price of leadership. Successful leaders adapt their behavior to meet group needs. Effective leaders in dynamic situations are positive, confident, and goal oriented. They have the ability to involve as many people as possible in the solution to organizational problems. Effective leaders stimulate motivation and ineffective leaders inhibit motivation. Consequently, an effective leader delegates. However, many leaders of the commander persuasion direct their organizations but misdirect people. Organizations can't be bossed into survival or success. The commander will put the welfare of his organization above the people. The true leader tries to make the two the same. Commanders direct by position power. Leaders guide by personal power. An editorial describing General Norman Schwarzkopf, of Desert Storm fame, had this to say, "Stormin' Norman Schwarzkopf stuck it to 'em: pulled off the swiftest, most one-sided, most decisive military operation in modern military annals – and didn't put a foot wrong."

Equally to his credit was his tender but intensely competent solicitude for the lives and well-being of his troops.

Whatever happens in the Persian Gulf from this point forward, America has a new national hero. A military hero, would you have believed it? –but one whose appeal and capabilities transcend military definitions.

Stormin' Norman is more than a good democratic soldier. He's a marvelous tonic for the grogginess that afflicts us in an age of self-seeking and egoism.

Here's a commander who knows exactly how to get from Point A to Point Z with maximum speed and efficiency. A commander, equally important, who puts his soldiers first.

The old military maxim is that the officer doesn't eat until the troops have been fed. Stormin' Norman, who in Vietnam once crossed a mine field to rescue a soldier with his leg half blown off, shows us the maxim lives.

What a model of leadership – actually leading instead of driving, herding, kicking, denigrating, disparaging, monopolizing credit, caring not a snap of the fingers for the grunts doing the heavy lifting.

He probably could run this country and do it well. I just don't know whether we'd want to inflict that on a man who's done so much for the country – and for all of us who call it home.[19]

The act of leading people is difficult to master, but for men and women like General Schwarzkopf it is not the car they drive, the house they live in, or the rank they wear but inner strength and the application of basic values that earns them the right to lead. If you want to determine if you are a leader or not, look around and see if anyone is following. You are as much a leader today as you are going to be because the price you are paying by your actions today is determining the kind of leader you will be tomorrow. Loneliness, weariness, abandonment, faith and vision are all a part of that price. True leadership exacts a toll in work, sweat, patience, faith and endurance. Leadership is not personality, it is not position or endowment, it is price. The leader is never more important than the body. To lead is a privilege that is granted by those that follow. The leader must be able to inspire those that follow because action must be sustained in order to achieve goals. Those that are led are quick to detect any lack of assurance, endurance or enthusiasm in the leader. Failure here will debilitate the leader in helping others emerge out of doubt and lack of confidence. Therefore, the best leaders have a clearly defined vision or dream and deep faith in the end results. Only deep faith manifested in the life of the leader results in the inspiration that people require. The faith and vision that he or she can get them from where they are to where they are going, faith and trust in the people and belief that they desire to be led empowers loyalty. All of these things tend to build people. The best leaders are people builders that offer hope and significance and growth. Without these things futility and pessimism run rampant. Leaders plan to grow, are open to new ideas and work with smarter people. They delegate authority and educate others and because personal growth can be discouraging they become people builders, helping them change and grow. This type of leadership has honesty and integrity at its cornerstone and trust as its foundation.

Leadership that works is leadership that inspires other people to action. This is the paradigm shift of the millennium, how well companies motivate and empower the people they employ. These leaders know the true power of an organization lies within its people. They are not threatened by giving away power and control. Rather, they have a high level of self-confidence and esteem not just from positional power. People must be inspired to new levels of creativity and innovation.

People want to be part of a winning team. Leadership shows up in the action of others. True leaders can make unreasonable requests of others and have them fulfilled, because people are inspired.

Servant leaders create leaders and call other leaders of like skills to service. It is interesting to note that the selection of the "right" leader ultimately infuses an organization with like-minded leaders. The Civil War ground on for years until Abraham Lincoln chose Ulysses S. Grant to lead. But it was Grant's selection of Sherman and Sheridan that ended the war in a year. In like manner, President Roosevelt chose George C. Marshall and President Truman, Dwight D. Eisenhower. General Marshall carried a list of top performers with him all through his career, ones he could call on if he needed them. Leaders duplicate themselves.

The core of the leadership council at Mail Boxes Etc. has been with me for many years. Peter Holt, our Vice President of International and I have been together for about 14 years. Peter studied abroad in Spain and worked on his MBA at the London School of Economics. He is one of the top transnationalists in the world. Tom Herskowitz, our Executive Vice President of Development, has a JD and an MBA in finance and was a "top gun" in Vietnam with over 300 combat missions. Lynn Lowder, our Executive Vice President & General Counsel, I also served with in Vietnam. Lynn won a silver star for bravery in combat with the United States Marines. These men are legitimate American heroes that have developed integrity and trust, formed and earned in the trenches. They are trustworthy because they have character and competence. They excel as a group because they don't care who gets the credit. That is servant leadership and it is being earned every day going forward with the fine men and women that make up the rest of the Leadership Team.

Real change comes from the inside out. The intention of leadership is at issue. Intention reflects who we really are. Our walk, gestures, body language, facial expressions, reactions, decisions, attitudes, relationships, people will perceive the real intention behind our actions and words in these ways. Servant leaders know that the hearts and minds of their people can be won when they are working toward a purpose they find worthwhile, are involved in the planning and decision making and feel appreciated by leadership. Servant leaders know that people will give their all in working together to accomplish their shared vision. Servant leaders appreciate people and want to help them grow and prosper as individuals.[20]

When setbacks do occur and what seems like insurmountable odds appear, the leader who refuses to admit defeat, who has a strong faith in himself to lead, confidence in his knowledge and powers of discernment will often carry the day. Such leaders often feel that leadership is their destiny and they derive great spiritual support from outside themselves. There are many times of extreme loneliness associated with effective leadership. People will betray the leader. Sometimes even those you think you can count on will fade away. Consequently, spiritual faith is a mandate even when the objectives are secular. The leader is an inseparable part of the group while at the same time not having the luxury of the deep social interaction of the group. Because leaders are empowered by influence, resources, the ability to give directions and prestige and reputation, conflict can result. How this is handled determines unity and loyalty in the organization. Problems with people must be handled quickly with the slightest amount of tension. Avoiding conflict is not the answer because that inhibits creativity, change and growth. People expect dedication, clear goals, persistence, ethics and openness. Leaders will offer diligence, integrity, attitude development, good relationship and purpose. Unfortunately, the general response to life is moping, doping, groping and hoping. We either cope or cop out. The difference is a powerful purpose instilled by a visionary leader. Invincible determination, do or die, win or lose all. Little plans, spread sheets and maximizing net present values do not stir the souls of men. Solid progress, solid success, solid answers are found in solid purpose.

Today we strive for leadership while organizations search for leaders. God and man are continually searching for leaders. John D. Rockefeller said he would pay more for the ability to deal with people than any other ability under the sun. That art of leadership is more important than intelligence, decisiveness, knowledge or effort. What it boils down to, like every other focus point we are discussing, is whether one is willing to pay the price and shoulder the responsibility to lead. The effective leader is indispensable. Without him or her there is no movement. The leader lights the coals of desire in others from his own inner fire. The requirements are hard work, faith, patience and endurance that always exact a toll on the individual. In fact, it is he or she that must set the high standards for others.

Fifteen or sixteen years ago, J. Oswald Soneley wrote about the true leader. I would like to share with you those qualities that I believe apply to today's transformational leader who is in pursuit of what Soneley called "the garland of amaranth," the goal promised in the Bible for the faithful leader.

The true (servant) leader:

is disciplined

has vision

is optimistic

has wisdom

makes decisions

has courage

is humble

has integrity

has humor

is a friend

is inspirational

has executive ability

is a listener

can write

inspired by God

prays

reads

pays the price

experiences loneliness and fatigue.

will be criticized

will be rejected

takes calculated risks

The servant leader strives for excellence but understands he can't do it all himself. Further, he knows that no matter what he does, there will be people who will not be pleased. Nonetheless, excellence comes, not from better programs, but from better people and people who are given the opportunity to become better. It is interesting to note that the higher you go in any growing organization, the better the attitude. It is competence that separates the winners from the losers. Many individuals in position of power substitute their authority for competence. There is no substitute for competence just as there is no substitute for excellence. There is no automatic transmission in a group that makes it run. It requires the know how and drive of someone who knows how to make it go. The best leaders have courses charted, goals set and objectives described.

One of the fundamental acts of leadership is to make people aware of what they feel. This was at the core of Mr. Perot's popularity when he began his quest for the presidency. He succeeded initially and eventually garnered 19 percent of the popular vote by enumerating needs people were feeling. This is what "transformational leadership" is all about. Great leaders help people to define their values and that alone will move them to action. People want to be patriotic, reverent and called to high ideals. It is renewal that is sought and ultimately it requires both substance and philosophy. All of us, at times find ourselves, lost, blind, stupid and scared. Articulating the vision and reminding people of the dream pulls from the past, relates to the present and offers a link to the future. This is the type of leadership that is at the beating heart of an organization sending its life-giving blood to the arteries.

Yet, the world is full of dying organizations, both profit and nonprofit, associations, churches, governments and even countries that are collapsing today, all because of ineffective leadership. America is no exception. The great financial losses to all types of organizations are mistakes in people selection. However, right up near the top are mistakes made in people application. Often talent is there but either misdirected or in the wrong place. Leaders must help people improve their talent, knowledge and skills. Too many times promotion is emphasized over development. If leadership is weak and fears competition from a subordinate or is afraid of losing recognition or perhaps revealing weakness, then development will not occur. An environment of life-long learning must be championed.

Confidence must permeate the group and it comes from the top. It is not what a leader thinks he is doing that counts, it is what those he is leading think he is doing that counts. Do not set your own price for success. Stay honest and disappointed with yourself. Don't let your ego get in the way. Create action, maintain integrity, work hard at acceptance of everyone, set the pace, maintain pride with humility and always reach the people. Offer trust, offer loyalty and recognize both the privilege and responsibility of leadership. Your witness to your business or organization or the people you lead begins with what you are, not with what you say. People notice what is happening, not things that aren't. The organization goes as the leader goes. People are looking for the leader. The right person that handles things right. That person lives on faith, not fear, and like garlic, it is a trust that projects and permeates the organization. A family, a church, a nation is only as strong as its leadership.

Leadership and influence are fundamental to everyone. The maximum investment is the investment we make in other people. Not sharing our riches with others but revealing to them their own. Remember the larger the rock dropped in a still pool the greater the ripples that radiate out. Our leadership and influence in life is exactly the same. Most of us do not have enough patience. We dump people because they have not lived up to our expectations not because they haven't performed well enough. People will follow a leader who is at the head of the line, not showing the way but leading the way. Not a sign post telling you what is ahead but a leader showing you how to get there. What motivates people is not money but vision, the dream and the provision of affirmation and encouragement. People are motivated when they feel a leader believes in them and cares about them personally. They don't care how much you know until they know how much you care. They are much more likely to follow and trust a leader if they know he or she is compassionate, understanding and forgiving.

Before the needle in a compass will respond to the pull of the north pole, it must be magnetized. Once it is magnetized it will never be the same again. Such it is with people. Multitudes unmagnetized, motionless and unresponsive. The effective leader is the magic. The effective leader is the element that magnetizes the needle. Knowledge itself does not motivate people to acceptable behavior. People are motivated by what they love, not by what they know. Regardless of what the rationalists of our time say, people follow their hearts and not their heads. They are imbued by a vision manifested by a leader to believe it, pursue it, and apprehend it. The message of the leader is projected through his or her own life. The greatest leaders are servants. Leaders who lead because they have been willing to follow. Because they offered faith and trust and loyalty they receive faith and trust and loyalty. This is the emotional glue that binds followers and leaders together. It involves risk, but it builds confidence and stimulates people to do their best.

Finally, servant leaders are heroes. They are men and women who are admired for their achievements and courage. They model excellence and have vision, determination, values and accountability. They do not suffer the politics of popularity but believe in what they do and then do what they believe. They are champions of the dream. They are servant leaders. **Focus on leadership.**

RECOMMENDED READING:

Four Star Leadership for Leaders: Jones & Ancell

Be The Leader You Were Meant To Be: Leroy Eims

Leadership Principles of Jesus: Bob Briner & Ray Pritchard

*There is no room in this country
for hyphenated Americanism . . .*

*The one absolutely certain way of
bringing this nation to ruin,
of preventing all possibility of
its continuing to be a nation at all,
would be to permit it to become
a tangle of squabbling nationalities.*

- Theodore Roosevelt

*Little happens in a relationship
until the individuals learn to trust each other.*

- David N. Johnson

VIII

FOCUS ON: RELATIONSHIP

All of us need help. All of us need friends in times of testing. Unless we feel needed by someone, life is meaningless. We are responsible for one another. Yet, the world is like a gigantic hospital where people suffer alone while the greatest healing therapy, love and friendship goes wanting. Loneliness has become the predominant attitude of our culture.

Why do we:

-Ask others into our life only to smother them in possessive attitudes?

-Want someone to care and then second guess their motives?

-Chastise others for indifference when it is us who authors isolation, selfishness and often cruelty?

-Think that to be somebody we must have somebody?

-Compulsively rush toward relationships and yet seek freedom?

-Point our fingers at others for letting us down when it is us who have been leaning on?

-Marry in anticipation only to have half end in divorce?

-Weep for the misfortune of friends while secretly harboring a smug satisfaction at their problem?

-Try to extract from others what we are incapable of bringing to them ourselves?

All of us need help. We need each other! Two cows grazing in a pasture saw a milk truck pass. On the side of the truck were the words, "Pasteurized, homogenized, standardized, vitamin A added." One cow sighed and said to the other, "makes you feel sort of inadequate, doesn't it?" We, too, are inadequate without quality, cooperative relationships. People are the supplement that make our life better. We are all imperfect human beings with imperfect relationships. Nobody has perfect love for friends and family. The truth is, as a result of the improper focus on I and me and my, most of us don't have relationships, we take hostages. Relationships begin with giving and receiving in a world where there are no guarantees. What we appear to want, however, is a risk free guaranteed environment, even in our relationships. But love and friendship and relationships that are guaranteed are not real. We try to maintain control when in reality we are dependent beings with no memory from where we came. Like the spider that slides down from his lofty heights to build and weave his web, one day we look up in wonder at the thin strand rising up and out of sight and in incomprehensible curiosity we yank at the thread and collapse our entire world. We cannot handle life on our own. Community is just that. Common unity. We need friends and friendship. We need to remember where we came from.

Bill Murchison commenting in the *Dallas Morning News* in October, 1991, said: "When we finally pried apart all those praying hands that give so much offense on public property, we should give thought to the public consequences of the dissolution of religious-based morality.

Is America's chief problem today a dearth of American Civil Liberties Union attorneys running around filing suits against school prayer? Or is it - much likelier - a general, and depressing, downturn in public morality, so that growing numbers today do what they want to do, when they want to do it, never mind the innocent people who get hurt? The moral tone of society is noticeably, and demonstrably, lower than was the case a few decades ago.

Indifference to higher standards of conduct, to the necessity of respecting others' rights and personhood, has spread throughout society. A "me"-oriented secular culture doesn't cotton to the idea of submission to external standards. It is just such standards that religion routinely and necessarily imposes. Religion says, look up. The culture says, look around; look at all the different and delightful ways we have for "expressing" ourselves. Religion points sadly but stubbornly to human imperfection, and to the resultant inadequacy of human efforts. Thus the command: Look up."[21]

There is a great emphasis on organizational and team building today. Organization occurs every time two or more people decide to carry out a task. So does relationship, incidentally. Life offers four basic relationships; God, other people, ourselves and things. I would submit this order is appropriate, but that discussion may be for another book. More importantly, we are born relational human beings. We grow desiring relationships and then wondering if they are worth the effort. Most people seem to be struggling to live effectively as relational human beings. Relationship is at the heart of all of our problems.

It is here in the heart of relationship that we first glimpse the final cure. It is also here that we find the hard questions largely unasked. I find it interesting, that the Bible has very little to say about organizational building or structure but a great deal to say about relationships. Yet the church is inhabited by people who in unspoken conspiracy deny the loneliness and emptiness and void that plague humanity. We have lost all claim to moral excellence, as we have seen with the Supreme Court confirmation hearings of Judge Clarence Thomas. We have politicized the norms of behavior. Sexual harassment as an example of an impaired relationship is serious. Only now it takes a Congresswoman to tell us that it is not funny, cute or complimentary. Activists now define what is right or wrong or politically correct or incorrect. Again, Murchison in the October 12, 1991 *Dallas Morning News* commented...

"Here is how it used to be. Male children, in common with female children, were taught observance, not of the latest sociological fad, but of the moral law, transcendent and abiding.

Churches and families did most of the teaching. This is not to say the teaching always "took," because it didn't. It is merely to say the teaching was offered, and that many, to society's immense profit, took it at least half seriously.

No robbing, no killing; respect the weak and helpless; do unto others as you would be done unto. No legislative body had enacted this enormous but simple code, based on mercy and respect. The code was inscribed plainly on minds and consciences. Legislators came along later to give it practical effect, as with the penalties for murder.

Sexual harassment, whatever it means or doesn't mean, is part of a far bigger picture, to which we should pay far closer attention.

The problem is the virtual disappearance of the moral law's old-time authority. Over time, "enlightened" people, having listened to philosophers and politicians, decided there wasn't any such animal as a moral law; why, it was all just a fabric of silly outdated, aristocratic prejudices. There probably wasn't a God anyway, and if there were he'd be sensible enough to let people do what they wanted. This great transformation in viewpoint began before Burke; it seems to have worked its way pretty near to consummation.

We haven't talked about the moral law in so long we've forgotten how wonderfully it once bound society together. Knocking it down, we were going to level out inequalities in society. In a pig's eye."[22]

Like loving, building relationships requires a decision that is based on our inconvenience not the inconvenience of other people. Just as a feeling of inadequacy always follows a lack of commitment to any worthy goal, so it is with relationships. We can refuse to commit to the point where we no longer recognize what is real and end up hating ourselves in the process.

A person simply cannot fight the world and find acceptance and achievement within it. Absolutely everyone has dependency needs. Yet, when we feel inadequate, we feel it is degrading to reach out for help. As children we are dependent. As teens, we are independent. As mature adults we should become interdependent. Interdependency requires caring. It takes courage to care. We know that love is the deepest human craving. That people will trade their time, money and virtue for it. It makes sacrifices appear to be simple and as many poets have reflected, the road is not too dark nor the night too long for genuine love. But the uncommitted lack love. True love is sustained by people who can sustain themselves independently. They choose to stay in the relationship. The best employees in any organization are volunteers because no matter how much they are paid they can leave any time they want. They stay because they love what they are doing. Love is at the center of all quality relationships.

Within the four basic relationships there are of course, many possible relationships. All relationships are important. But it appears that once again we have strayed from the fundamentals and may not be listening to the right voices today. At particular risk is the home, with husband and wife and children relationships suffering. If one listens to the media or is merely a casual observer the conclusion that is drawn is that the family and marriage has had it. If so, we should be doubly concerned because there has never been a nation that has survived the disintegration of the home.

Our children are not being provided a definition of unconditional love within the home because the role models are incapable of expressing this type of commitment. Nothing typifies the level of unconditional love more than a moving song Harry Chapin wrote shortly before his tragic death. He entitled this song, *Cats in the Cradle:*

My child arrived just the other day.

He came to the world in the usual way.

But there were planes to catch and bills to pay.

He learned to walk while I was away.

And he was talkin' 'fore I knew it and as he grew

He'd say "I'm gonna be like you, Dad,

You know I'm gonna be like you."

And the cat's in the cradle and the silver spoon.

Little boy blue and the man on the moon.

"When you comin' home, Dad?"
"I don't know when, but we'll get together then.
You know we'll have a good time then."

My son turned ten just the other day.
He said "Thanks for the ball, Dad, come on, let's play,
Can you teach me to throw?" I said "not today
I got a lot to do." He said "That's O.K."
And he walked away, but his smile never dimmed.
And said "I'm gonna be like him, yeah
You know I'm gonna be like him."

And the cat's in the cradle and the silver spoon.
Little boy blue and the man on the moon.
"When you comin' home, Dad?"
"I don't know when, but we'll get together then.
You know we'll have a good time then."

Well he came home from college just the other day
So much like a man I just had to say
"Son, I'm proud of you; can't you sit for a while?"
He shook his head and said with a smile
"What I'd really like, Dad, is to borrow the car keys.
See you later. Can I have them please?"

And the cat's in the cradle and the silver spoon.
Little boy blue and the man on the moon.
"When you comin' home, Dad?"
"I don't know when, but we'll get together then.
You know we'll have a good time then."

I've long since retired. My son's moved away.
I called him up just the other day.
I said "I'd like to see you if you don't mind."

He said, "I'd love to, Dad, if I can find the time.

You see my new job's a hassle and the kids have the flu.

But it's sure nice talking to you, Dad

`It's been sure nice talking to you."

And as I hung up the phone it occurred to me–

He'd grown up just like me.

My boy was just like me.

And the cat's in the cradle and the silver spoon.

Little boy blue and the man on the moon.

"When you comin' home, son?"

"I don't know when, but we'll get together then.

You know we'll have a good time then."

I don't know about you but the words of that song convict me. It reminds me of my own selfishness in almost every relationship I have ever had. In more lucid moments, I deeply regret the pain I have caused those I love the most because I failed to see truth and act on it.

With an emphasis on selfishness and power, the I, me, and my mentality have adopted an attitude of using people and loving things instead of loving people and using things. It appears that we run into trouble when our basic relationships lose their proper order or priority. We must change the world by changing our world. As we have discussed with each fundamental, it is the individual that must get back to the basics. The question is not whether marriage as an institution will survive or whether the family will survive. The real question, is will my marriage survive? Will my family relationship survive? J. Allen Petersen commenting in *Homemade* made this observation, "Most people get married believing a myth-that marriage is a beautiful box full of all the things they have longed for: companionship, sexual fulfillment, intimacy, friendship. The truth is that marriage, at the start, is an empty box. You must put something in before you can take anything out. There is no love in marriage; love is in people, and people put it into marriage. There is no romance in marriage; people have to infuse it into their marriages.

A couple must learn the art and form the habit of giving, loving, serving, praising-keeping the box full. If you take out more than you put in, the box will empty."

We counsel, probe, discuss, fret and worry about the problems of communication, money, sex, in-laws, rearing children and many other things. But they are only the symptoms of failed relationships not the disease that destroyed them. This is all part of the process of becoming. It is part of the journey, the quest that we are on to be real. It is a maturing of attitude that ultimately improves all relationships.

At the heart of failed relationships, is the emotion of loneliness. Loneliness may be the most desolate word in the human language. Often silent and destructive as a flooding river in the night, it leaves its slimy banks only to crest in the mud of despair. There is simply no other anguish like the consummating anguish of loneliness. Ask:

Any soldier thousands of miles away from home

Someone who has just buried their life's companion

A couple who loses a child

The single person that makes supper alone, leaves for work alone and knows they will come home to nothing that night.

Liza Girzartes pointed out that the world is full of lonely people, each isolated in a private secret dungeon.

One of the most booming businesses in America today is the 900 phone call numbers. Not necessarily for phone sex as you might imagine, but overwhelmingly used by people who are willing to pay money just to have someone else listen to them or talk to them. Relationships!

You and I were created with a soul and spirit for fellowship with God. While there is a difference in being alone and lonely, God never intended us to be lonely in our hearts. There are three billion people on earth today but there is a greater sense of loneliness than ever before. You may be sitting surrounded by people as you read this but, for all practical purposes, are alone in the deepest desires of your heart, crying out for someone to love you, to recognize you, to listen to you. Loneliness is not geography, it is attitude.

If you stop and think about it, the very words of new age thinking emphasizing the I, the me and the my, precludes the we, the us and the our, implicitly rejecting family and relationship. One of the consequences of loneliness is immorality. People are smothered and threatened by lousy relationships and loneliness that accompanies them so that they can't stand to be alone. They can't walk into an empty house without switching on the T.V. or the radio or anything that would assist in avoiding being reminded of the desolation in their lives. There is just no one to say "Hi" to, or "I love you" or "I missed you" or "here is lunch" or "I have been thinking about you." There is just nobody there.

Children turn to immorality when love isn't there. Eight or eighty we need relationships. We need to be loved. Often people who are just divorced feel the lack of fellowship and relationships. Where do they go? Who invites them? People everywhere are dying inside because they are lonely without relationships. The only thing that could possibly be worse would be not to have a relationship with God. How much more does the lonely person suffer without God in their heart? People want someone else to care but someone else is too absorbed with their own lives to even listen. Too often, they have had their beer and gone to bed. When we reject one another, we violate the very purpose for which we were born. Do you know what it means not to be wanted?

Why are there so many people that experience a loneliness that divides the mind and burdens the heart? Why do hundreds of thousands of kids get into trouble? Why are there so many old folks in rest homes surrounded by people but ready to die? Why are so many families being rent asunder, leaving aching expanses in the debris of shattered relationships? Why are so many people who are suffering discouragement and tragedy and loss faced with no one to whom they can open their hearts?

The unfortunate truth is-because few people really care. The world nods its head in recognition at best. The Church boasts of souls brought to Christ while often brushing aside lonely people in its path. People need friends. They need someone to listen. They need someone to care. They need someone to love. So do you. So do I. So does the person right next to you. Right now.

No one becomes lonely overnight. And lest you are tempted to whisk this relational fundamental away with a flick of your wrist, let me remind you that while you may stand tall, make monumental decisions that affect thousands of people or feel absolutely immortal, the world bowing down to you, a moment will come in your life when your family fades away and fear grips your heart knowing that the last step is to be made and the final foe faced. The one thing you do not want to do is to die without a relationship with God.

The loneliest place in the world is a heart without love. Just as real love cannot be given away without receiving it, real friendship cannot be offered without experiencing it. Solid, effective, mutually respectful relationships build. They do not destroy. As John Naisbitt noted in *Megatrends*, the more technical our society becomes the more we will have the need for human activities–the nurturing of arts and culture, a renewed emphasis on relationships, and a commitment of spiritual pursuits. Man is nothing outside of a vital relationship with God. Every profession or relationship in life will be tested whether with God, others, ourselves or things. There is no worse pain than a life void of meaningful relationships. Consequently, like the winter porcupine, we attempt to get close enough for warmth but not close enough to stick each other. With manipulative, self-protective and unloving motives, we negotiate for position.

To others we say: you want love, earn it. You want forgiveness, show me you deserve it. We entrap others in legalism and snare them with the same rule-ridden perfectionism that the church or our parents manipulated us. In this spirit of legalism and a pervasive secularism, we mistrust God, we mistrust others and we mistrust ourselves. The ultimate result of all of this is a fake moralism that embraces guilt in a mad rush from freedom. In the August 12, 1991, issue of the *Economist* the editors were compelled to write:..."a decadent Puritanism within America: We are breeding a sort of civic stupidity that brings with it the immobility of addiction. When the glue of society breaks down, old tolerances and civilities fall away along with concepts such as self-reliance and responsibility. We are living in the age of the "crybaby" or the all purpose victim, as TIME magazine points out. We have all become victims with the American dream no longer a privilege but now a right or an entitlement. And, in an environment of self-absorbed individualism, we forget that society cannot operate if everyone has rights and no one has responsibilities. The Marxist philosopher Herbert Marcuse in his treatise *One-Dimensional Man* argued that tolerance for the expression of intolerant attitudes, like racial discrimination, should be repressed for society's good. So now, we have intolerance being expressed through corporate lifestyle police who want to know if you are smoking at home with a neo-prohibitionist movement that is against almost anything, while imposing on others arbitrary standards of behavior, health and thought. They have lost sight of America. They have lost sight of tolerance. They are reflected in the face of the politically correct that have invaded academia. They are neo-Puritans that contribute to a self-centered moralism that is unprecedented in American history, and they rise at a time when the common values of our society are weak. This is not coincidence. Aided by the press, these people practice moral terrorism."[23]

What we need is a fundamental relationship based on old values. What we need are proper priorities and trust as the basis for all real relationships. Free to be hopeful, joyful, compassionate and forgiving, we recognize our own need and are able to translate that into the needs of others. Recognizing that we are far from being the type of person we would like to be, we are able to tolerate the inconsistencies of others. Trust at its basis, forgiveness at its heart, relationship then knows the towering freedom of love and forgiveness. **Focus on relationships.**

RECOMMENDED READING:

Spirit Controlled Temperament: LaHaye

Bringing Out The Best In People: McGinnis

Skill With People: Giblin

*Nothing greater can happen to a human being
than that he be forgiven.*

*And there can be no great love of things, ideas, or persons
without an understanding of the central, ethical role
that forgiveness should play in human affairs. . .
Pure forgiveness is unconditional it exacts no tribute,
requires no moral barter, Forgiveness is the divine
answer to every question implied in human existence,
for we all, all of us, are creatures who are fallible.*

*This is why no man can truly love
unless he accepts forgiveness as a way of life.*

*For the deeper our experience of forgiveness,
the greater our love.*

- Rabbi Stuart E. Rosenberg

IX

FOCUS ON: FORGIVENESS

Have you been hurt?

Has somebody somewhere in your past rejected you in such a way that you still hurt when you think about it?

Do you become critical of other people the minute their name is mentioned?

Did you leave home as a young person or college student with great relief that you were leaving?

Have you worked hard all your life not to become like your parents?

Are there people in your past upon whom you would enjoy taking revenge?

Were you abused as a child? Maybe even molested?

Did you suffer through your parent's divorce as a child? Were your parents taken from you when you were very young?

Were you forced by circumstances to pursue a different career from the one you originally wanted?

Were you unable to attend the school of your choice for financial reasons?

Were you pushed out of a job opportunity by a greedy friend?

Were you promised things by your employer that never came true?

Because we continue to do things that require forgiveness, there are no enduring relationships without forgiveness. In fact, forgiveness is the foundation of all continuous relationships. It is inextricably tied to love and is equally misunderstood and abused. Unfortunately, this reflects societal values that further demonstrate just how far we have run to escape truth and reason in America. The fundamentals of love and forgiveness have just as much application to business as attitude and leadership. And attitude and leadership are equally applicable to life. Hopefully, we are learning that each fundamentals is part of the tapestry we weave that becomes the warp and woof of life. They are principles. This is at the heart of why we need to get back to basics. Theories are of little use. Like pigeons they circle overhead endangering us with "fallout" when they fail. Principles, the fundamentals, apply to every area of life. They encompass truth. Truth has authority. Not over other truth, but over error. The authority of the fundamentals we are discussing lie in their truthfulness not where they come from or who happens to espouse them.

We have become a litigious society because of our inability to love and forgive. Once again, this reflects our priorities and values. I have had the good fortune to travel the world many times over as the chief executive officer of multi-national companies. I have found most of the world stands with mouth agape at the size of American legal documents and the lack of trust they demonstrate. In Japan, as an example, the majority of business agreements are done with only a handshake. Furthermore, only 6% of all of their disagreements are ever litigated. Unfortunately, as the Japanese have had to deal more and more with America, their legal documents become larger and larger. A case in point is occuring as I write these words. It is late July 1998 and at Mail Boxes Etc. we have been locked in tedious negotiations with one of the largest retailers in Japan for over a year now. We have been examining each word of a long and complicated document that has threatened to break off discussions of a relationship that would clearly be beneficial to both companies. Just a few years ago that would never have happened.

I know that there are hard-nosed business men and women reading these words laughing to themselves knowing that you must "cover your rear" with legal documents to succeed. I do not disagree. I simply make the observation, how sad. I have been thrilled, however, to make friends around the world. And I will tell you that while our companies also don the armor of our legal documents, every relationship we have developed in expanding internationally has been built on trust. Further, it is not the written agreement that has driven our growth but a mutual willingness to live up to the unwritten elements of each agreement. What are these unwritten elements? Mutual respect, trust, the right attitude, effective leadership and yes, even love and forgiveness. Why is forgiveness fundamental? Oscar Wilde said "we should forgive our enemies because there is nothing that annoys them quite so much." Phyllis Diller, another great modern philosopher once observed "Why go to bed angry when you can stay up and fight?" These two observations, while humorous, may in fact reflect the majority view of forgiveness. Tragically, this attitude is far off the mark. It is quite possible that there is no other fundamental save love when misunderstood and misused wreaks more havoc on humanity.

Without a doubt there is a spiritual element to the forgiveness. However, that is true for every fundamental of life. It is not my purpose here to discuss religion or dogma or proselytize. As I stated in the introduction, it is my purpose to provoke you to think. However, the journey I am taking has led me down a spiritual road. I believe that the most grievous error made as a result of the majority of advice and instruction proffered in life, has resulted in most of the time treating the symptoms and not the disease. By this, I mean that we too often leave out the whole person. Men and women are spirits that possess a soul and lives in a body. The treatment of the physical or mental, medically or psychologically, that eliminates any part of the whole person is doomed to failure. It is for that reason, that there is still so much heartbreak and pain after so much instruction. Such is the case with forgiveness. A Sunday school teacher once asked a little boy, "How do you receive forgiveness?" His response was, "First you have to sin." And so it is. Because you and I are born into sin we come into this world with a need for forgiveness. Because we have a bent relationship with God, our flesh feels guilt while only in the spirit can we be healed.

Forgiveness is absolutely essential to well-being in life. Forgiveness for you and me and others. I've heard it said that we are like beasts when we kill, like men when we judge but like God when we forgive. Forgiveness is the key that unlocks the door of resentment and the handcuffs of hate. It is a power that breaks the chains of bitterness and the shackles of selfishness.

The lack of forgiveness becomes a dark cloud that hangs over the head of many people. As Josh McDowell says, "When I refuse to forgive I am becoming a bridge that someday I will need to pass over." Suppose you were to grow up in a home where, no matter how hard you tried, you were never sure you had your father's approval. No matter how hard you tried, you still had to ask yourself the question, is my father displeased or not. Maybe you grow to adulthood and leave home still never sure that you had your father's approval. The result of all of this is a bondage that might last for the rest of your life. In fact, for many people that is exactly what happens. There is never a sense of intimacy between father and child. The dark cloud hangs there because there is always a sense of guilt of not measuring up or never knowing the joy of his love and acceptance. How important is it incidentally, to approve your child? To hug your child? To love your child?

This internal guilt and feeling of rejection is not only the lot of many people but most certainly, on a spiritual level, it describes what I believe are the majority of relationships between man and God the Father. Am I guilty? I always feel so guilty. I must be guilty. The point is, most of us are still capable of knowing the difference between right and wrong. For there to be guilt, there must be knowledge of guilt. For there to be knowledge of guilt there must be moral consciousness. For there to be moral consciousness there must be accountability and responsibility.

As children, we know when we do wrong. When we act on something that is wrong, we know that we will be held accountable. Exactly the same thing is true spiritually, it's just that as we grow older we often become too sophisticated and intellectual for the truth. Oh yes, we still carry the baggage of guilt and lack of forgiveness but somewhere along the way, just as many people do with their earthly father, we run away from God or we simply make excuses for our failures. We rationalize our failing and attendant guilt by self-talk such as, my childhood situation was bad or I just haven't had the opportunities others have had. The reason I don't measure up is because I don't measure up. My background is bad. I've had too many setbacks. I'm the wrong color to survive in this prejudiced environment. I'm too young or too old or too tall or too short or too fat or too thin. However, when you and I consent to do what we know is wrong whether in business, marriage or any other situation where we have identified ourselves with what we know is evil, then we are accountable.

When asked to describe if they had ever seen Billy Graham angry, Cliff Barrow described a situation very early in the ministry in Modesto, California. Billy had finished preaching and was stepping down off of the podium when a woman rushed up and embraced and kissed him. Billy apparently was very agitated, stating that the staff should never allow that type of thing to happen again. Out of this came what would be known as the "Modesto Manifesto". Billy and his trusted confidants agreed to hold themselves accountable to one another. To his credit, he knew that the very appearance of impropriety could be lethal. He did not want any possibility of identifying himself or his ministry with what might be construed as wrong.

Sin or wrong doing is a destroyer by nature. Why can't we learn that when we do things that we are ashamed of, and we all do, that it changes us inside and we begin to carry that negative baggage around. How can we pick up tomorrow if we are carrying yesterday in our arms? There are only two choices. One is to be able to go through life without error. The other is to be able to receive forgiveness, to be able to forgive ourselves and to be able to forgive others. You and I get off track when we try to make our way apart from what we know is right or more fundamentally, apart from God's admonitions. After the Gulf War, President Bush addressed a joint session of Congress. I found myself quite moved listening to the President as he described American soldiers reaching out in compassion to Iraqi prisoners of war as they emerged from their bunkers trembling and crying in fear. One American soldier, trying to comfort these pitiful and fearful men was heard to say to the surrendering Iraqis, "It's OK, you are all right now." There is obvious compassion and immediate forgiveness in his words and actions. The President commenting on this went on to say that America is a land of peace and compassion and values. What great leadership and how insightful. The knee jerk reaction of many people to such a statement is derision and cynicism, particularly in the face of the moral climate in America today. But exhorting people to look up to higher ideals and to stretch toward moral excellence does not obviate our failures. It simply reminds us of the dream. As William Faulkner said..."I believe man will not merely endure; he will prevail. He is immortal, not because he, alone among creatures, has an inexhaustible voice but because he has a soul, a spirit, capable of compassion and sacrifice and endurance." The poet's, the writer's duty is to write about these things. It is his privilege to help man endure by lifting his heart, by reminding him of courage and honor, hope and pride, compassion and pity and sacrifice. The poet's voice need not merely be the record of man, it can be one of the props, the pillars to help him endure and prevail.[24] Poet, politician, writer, economist, musician, producer all should recognize their duty in such a mission. Consequently, this type of leadership has nothing to do with partisan politics, it has everything to do with what Alexis d'Toqueville said many years ago after he visited the United States seeking the seeds of America's greatness. "America will be great as long as America is good." He understood that true freedom comes from moral strength and obedience that is rooted in trust. Many years later, General George C. Marshall being honored in 1953 as the recipient of the Nobel Peace Prize, forecasted the eventual and recent collapse of Communism when he said..."Tyranny inevitably must retire before the tremendous moral strength of the gospel of freedom and self-respect for the individual. We have to recognize that these democratic principles do not flourish on empty stomachs. However, material assistance alone is not sufficient. The most important thing for the world today is a spiritual regeneration that would establish a feeling of good faith among men generally." That "good faith among men generally" is what d'Toqueville understood to be at the root of the miracle of America. As General Marshall prophesied forty years ago, without adherence to real basics Communism itself would collapse. What will happen to America without continued focus on such fundamentals. Additional insight is offered by William Fairlie writing in *The New Republic*. "The desire for a risk-free society is one of the most debilitating influences in America today, enfeebling the economy with a mass of safety regulations and a fear of liability rulings.

Of course there is such a thing as a level of risk that is unacceptable. But in America the threshold of tolerable risk has been set so low that the nation is refusing to pay the inevitable costs of human endeavor.

If America's new timorousness had prevailed among the Vikings, their ships with the bold prows but frail hulls would have been declared unseaworthy. The Norsemen would have stayed home and jogged."[25]

Violating the laws of God and man will not buy security, it won't meet your needs, it won't satisfy and it won't bring contentment, happiness or peace. Remember you can't carve rotten wood. We must get this right. Since we are incapable of living an error free life, there must be forgiveness or we end up living our lives under a cloud of displeasure. The practical application of this on a daily basis is most important. The spiritual repercussions are monumental and eternal. Forgiveness is a matter of life and death. In fact to receive Divine forgiveness is to receive a life right now that knows no end.

In his book, *The Autobiography of God*, Lloyd Ogilvie made the comment that there is a stupidity of independence all of us want to be what we can never be, Lord over our own lives. In the fifteenth chapter of Luke, in the New Testament of the Bible, there is a parable about a lost son. I want to use this story as an illustration of the fundamental because it best depicts God's attitude about forgiveness and might be able to help us understand what our own attitude should be. Whether you are Christian or not, this is a powerful principle. The audience listening to Jesus tell the story were the tax gatherers or Publicans of the day along with the scribes and Pharisees. The Prodigal Son of this story was the perfect example for this group. He was the younger son of a household who wanted his part of his estate and he wanted to leave. This was a tragic failing on the part of the family and of the father in particular. The boy left and squandered and wasted his inheritance on immoral indulgences in a far away country. A severe famine occurred and he began to be in great need. As we previously discussed when we violate God's laws and principles, when we lose sight of the fundamentals, we can expect famine in our lives as individuals and in our nation. Next, this young man did the most despicable thing that a young Jewish boy could do. He went to feed swine or pigs and not only that, but he wanted to eat the same food that the pigs were eating. This really hit the Pharisees who were listening, in the face. Remembering our focus on relationship, you can't help but wonder, incidentally, what happened to all this young man's friends who were there when he had money.

The real point to be made here, however, is that God's motivation for forgiveness is in Himself. This young man's actions left nothing to motivate a desire to forgive. Like many of us, he stumbled home from waste and wandering to survive. His rush toward "freedom" became an escape from freedom, friends gone, wine soured, the glitter of the far country dulled beyond recognition he came face to face with bondage, despair and his own mortality. He wasn't even coming home with pure motives, money gone, he just wanted to survive. Nonetheless, his father took him back just as he was. God's forgiveness is not based on performance or conduct or even promise, it is based on love and so it should be for us. In the story, the boy decides to return home because he figures his father's servants are living a better life than he is with the pigs. His father, when he sees him returning, runs out and hugs and kisses him. Actually, what the Pharisees hear is that God is running out after a pig slopper. No one ran in public in those days because it was considered undignified. This was a further affront to their sensibilities. The father ran out to meet his wayward son with no requirement to account for the money and no lecture on immorality. There was only an attitude of patient, loving, complete and total forgiveness. Actually, whether he recognized it or not, the prodigal son came home to get forgiveness. His father's attitude, as we have stated, was not one of waiting on the porch demanding an accounting and payment that might last a lifetime. Oh no! He ran down the road, put a ring and a cloak on his son and had a party, rejoicing in the return and the healing of the relationship. Incidentally, that young man was forgiven before he even committed wrong or sin in his life.

Meanwhile, his older brother became angry. He was angry at his father because while he remained busy with his father's work and did not squander his inheritance, his brother, the Prodigal, chose to leave and squandered his portion. Yet, here was his father welcoming his brother home as if nothing had happened. The older brother was in concert with his father's work but not in harmony with his father's heart. He did not have the same attitude as his father. Why is it important for us to be able to forgive as well as receive forgiveness? Suppose that young man had met his brother first when he returned home and not his father. What do you think would have happened? How many times do you and I meet the "elder brother" in life when we desperately need the enfolding arms of the loving father? Worse still, how many times have we been the elder brother, when our son or daughter or wife or husband or mother or father or friend needed our understanding love and instead got lost in a labyrinth of legalism and the hardness of our heart. God forgive me for those poignant times when I looked down the long nose of piety at my daughters when they erred. Needing love and understanding, I offered instruction and sanctimonious moralism. In the deepest corners of my being, out of the winter of my soul, I ask their forgiveness for the lack of forgiveness in my own heart.

I have heard from people who raise turkeys that if a turkey sees a spot of blood on another turkey he will pick at that spot until he literally kills the object of his attention. I know I have been like that, at times. I still struggle with being critical. Irving Wallace in The Pearl demonstrates this same attitude by illustrating that if a blemish on a pearl is rubbed and picked at long enough, there will be nothing left. Not even the good. Thomas Wolf in *The Return of The Native* said you can never go home again. The truth is we can. This doesn't mean that we do not suffer the consequences of wrong actions in our lives. The Prodigal Son wasted time, talent, resources, gifts and life. That leaves scars. Forgiveness does not always erase the scars but it does offer a new beginning.

Forgiveness is one of the untapped and least understood sources of all healing power. Wrong actions, evil intent and sin produce fear, doubt and uncertainty. In addition, we place ourselves in bondage when we fail to forgive someone else. There is simply no such thing as a happy, joyful person with an unforgiving spirit. Physiologically, the body responds to what the mind and the spirit feel. The entire body feels the tension of an unforgiving spirit, consequently, forgiveness is a paradox because it appears contradictory to our own self interests to let go of wrongs.

Yet, an unforgiving spirit is the primary cause of many health problems. It increases stress, harming the body, mind, emotions, families, relationships, life work, ambition and desire. It is a poison that may have been for weeks, months or even years. There is no way to harbor an unforgiving spirit without it corroding and disintegrating something inside of us. It is devastating and collapsing and must be dealt with if we are to heal emotionally, mentally and spiritually. Some people get married on the heels of a relationship full of bitterness and resentment and bring that same spirit into the new relationship never realizing that it cannot be contained if not released. You cannot love with a heart full of unforgiveness. When we begin to build walls between us and another person we also build walls that shut out other people. In fact, this attitude can be passed on from generation to generation. A parent who's emotion, will and mind are paralyzed because of bitterness and unforgiveness cannot love, even if they want to. There are parents who wonder why they can't love their children and children who wonder why they can't love their parents and husbands and wives who can't understand why everything that comes from deep inside them is negative, distrustful, insecure and resentful. All of these relationships can be healed if we would only realize that forgiveness means our willingness to bear the loss and suffer the hurt, to be understanding and ultimately to love. This requires time and healing. The capacity to enjoy and experience this type of forgiveness depends on our attitude. I believe that if we could ever understand just an inkling of God's love and forgiveness for us, we would find it extremely difficult to hold that healing balm back from others. Like everyone else, we fail. Jerked around by the inconsistency of our own emotions, bruised and battered by rejection and lapses we often wander the far country. While seeking freedom, we opt for slavery and imprison ourselves in the desires for things we ultimately end up hating. Yet, Thomas Wolfe was wrong. We can go home. We don't even have to analyze our intention. Thank God, we don't have to be perfect and we don't ever have to wallow in deep despair. We can even come home with a secret longing for the far country. I don't think I have ever heard the church speak to that. The truth is that in the face of repentance many of us have had a secret fondness for some of the "fun" experienced in sin. This is not to diminish the necessity or power of repentance. But, it is true that to a degenerate man, many of Satan's lies seem a lot more logical and satisfying in the short term than the long term results of God's truth. That is part of why the attraction for the far country is so powerful and forgiveness is fundamental to life.

An unforgiving spirit sends us to our grave having been cheated and deprived of friends, intimate relationships and inner peace and joy. Hell was often described in the Bible as Gehenna in the Valley of Hinnon where garbage was dumped day and night in ancient times. It was a place of wasted lives, where lives were never invested but only spent, where there were never any meaningful relationships. This is the place of unforgiveness. **Focus on forgiveness.**

RECOMMENDED READING:

Autobiography of God: Lloyd Ogilive

Love, Acceptance & Forgiveness: Cook, Jerry & Baldwin

Forgiveness: Charles Stanley

We are shaped and fashioned by what we love.

- Goethe

The way to love something is to realize it might be lost.

- G. K. Chesterson

X

FOCUS ON: LOVE

Of all the words that are more misused, abused, and misunderstood, there is no word like the word "love". Of all life's focus points none that is more misapplied, misdirected and ill-received than love. Of all the great needs of America and humanity, the greatest is to be loved. Not selfish, immoral or irresponsible love but a love that bestows no greater feeling of self-worth than when it is given or received. It converts hate, it changes tragedy into triumph, tears into joy and it is our greatest challenge. We are all guilty of failing to love. One of the stories that circulated in the Marine Corps back in 1969 when I was in Vietnam, was of a young Marine Johnny Simmons, that had stopped at Travis Air Force Base on his way home from Vietnam. There, he placed a call to his parents to ask them if they would mind if he would bring home a friend who had lost an arm, a leg and one eye in combat. His parents, uncomfortable facing such a homecoming, suggested that another time might be more appropriate. Several times this young man repeated his desire to bring his friend home but his parents still were resistant and clearly uncomfortable. Sadly, he agreed that maybe they were right and saying good-bye he hung up. That night, he took his life because while it was his own arm and leg and eye that had been shattered in combat, it was his heart that had been shattered upon returning home. Undoubtedly, his parents would have offered unconditional love had they but known he was talking about himself. I wonder how many times you and I place conditions on our acceptance and our love of others not realizing the pain and destruction we reap in their lives. As I wrote in *The Memorial*, Crown Books, 1989, I believe this same rejection on the part of America toward our Vietnam veterans was responsible for much of the anxiety and depression that frustrated a generation of youth from finding their rightful and responsible place in society. Unfortunately, it is very difficult to give away what we have never received and many people have never received unconditional love. It is not easy to love. Love flows like a spring. It is never stagnant, always giving. It is not what most people think it is, merely a feeling or an emotion. It is learned. It is not always convenient but it wins every single time. You and I can feel all kinds of things but genuine, unconditional, selfless love is a decision. When at the altar, we say "I take thee to be my lawfully wedded wife/husband, to live together in a holy state of matrimony, to love you, comfort you, honor you, keep you in sickness and in health, to death do us part", that is not a feeling being expressed but rather a decision being made. A covenant being entered into with you, your spouse and God. If you are waiting to fall in love, you may have a problem. Not only can we learn to love and make a quality decision to love but, just as obviously, many people who think they fall in love find themselves getting to a place in their lives where they have made a decision to no longer love.

Love can be learned and like other attitudes it is a result of what we think, feel and do. It is a result of understanding. In Forrest Carter's fine book *The Education of Little Tree*, Little Tree is talking. "Granma's name was Bonnie Bee. I knew that when I heard him late at night say I kin ye, Bonnie Bee,' he was saying, I love ye,' for the feeling was in the words.

And when they would be talking and Granma would say, Do ye kin me, Wales?' and he would answer, I kin ye,' it meant, I understand ye.' To them, love and understanding was the same thing. Granma said you couldn't love something you didn't understand; nor could you love people, nor God, if you didn't understand the people and God.

Granpa and Granma had an understanding, and so they had a love. Granma said the understanding run deeper as the years went by, and she reckined it would get beyond anything mortal folks could think upon or explain. And so they called it kin.'

Granpa said back before his time kinfolks' meant any folks that you understood and had an understanding with, so it meant loved folks.' But people got selfish, and brought it down to mean just blood relatives; but that actually it was never meant to mean that."

In another example of the relationship between love and understanding, suppose you were driving to work on a busy freeway in the morning. Traffic is backed up for miles and it is already very hot. Your air conditioner is broken, traffic is at a standstill and the guy behind you leans on his horn. After a few minutes, you might exit your car to go back and at the very least give this individual a few cogent observations about his behavior. But, as you approach the car the driver leans out of the window and tells you that he was just notified that his child was near death at the hospital and he needs to get there as fast as possible. All of a sudden your behavior changes. Instead of becoming part of the problem you now want to be part of the solution. In fact, you might try to get out and direct traffic out of the way. The point is, like other attitudes love is multi-dimensional. What you once thought about that person and the emotions associated with that line of thinking are now gone. In fact, the action you were about to take is also dramatically altered. Now, because you understand that person's behavior, you accept it. Further, because you accept the behavior you are now willing to get involved and that is what love really is all about. Understanding, acceptance and involvement. A story in *Our Daily Bread* further illustrates this point. Many years ago, a professor at the University of Edinburgh was listening to his students as they presented oral readings. One young man rose to begin his recitation but was abruptly stopped by the professor, "you are holding the book in the wrong hand," criticized the educator. "Take your book in the right hand and be seated."

Responding to this strong rebuke, the young man held up his right arm. He didn't have a right hand! The other students were deathly quiet and began to shift in their seats. For a moment the professor sat in dumbfounded silence. Then he slowly made his way to the student, put his arm around him and with a tear in his eye, said "I am so sorry. I never knew. Please, will you forgive me?"

Once again, understanding behavior resulted in acceptance and the loving balm of forgiveness. We have forgotten how to live in America. Bombarded and blasted with advertising that tells us to love everything from Coke to the fact that we should use our spiritual power of prayer to pray for beer, we are admonished to look out for number one and wear the right clothes to earn acceptance and love. All of this is wrapped in a cynicism unprecedented in America, lusting for what love truly represents.

Dale Galloway, commenting on the transforming miracle of real love made the following comments.

A great example of one who related out of love instead of our of fear was Father Damien, a courageous Roman Catholic missionary, who, from 1873 to 1889, worked for God in a leper colony. The colony was located on the Hawaiian Island of Molokai.

A recent television program told the story, beginning with Father Damien's arrival by ship. Before the missionary got off the ship, the captain, with a scornful laugh, told him he wouldn't stay long in the leper colony but, like all other clergymen, would return soon to the ship.

As the priest prepared to step from the large ship to a small rowboat that would take him ashore, the leper at the oars held out his hand to help the priest into the boat. Seized by the fear of leprosy, the priest refused the man's hand. Hurt and separation showed in the leper's eyes as he held out the oar for the priest to grasp.

Arriving at the colony, Father Damien found his church building in shambles and his congregation nonexistent. The lepers wanted nothing to do with him and his touch-me-not brand of Christianity. The priest beat on the bell to summon people to the church, but the lepers turned deaf ears to all his pleas and calls.

Beaten and giving up, Father Damien made his way back to the ship, which had returned to the colony. On board, however, something happened that changed his life and would literally transform the leper colony.

A load of lumber intended for another Catholic parish was on board. Seeing it, the priest demanded that the captain drop the lumber off here for the lepers. The captain refused.

Also on board was a fresh band of untouchable lepers to be dropped at the colony. Father Damien, caught up in a cause greater than himself, forgot about his fear and in love, picked up a little girl who had leprosy. Holding her close, he gently kissed her little cheek. Then he threatened the captain that unless he lowered the lumber and left it for the leper colony, the little girl would kiss him. The fearful captain immediately agreed to the priest's demand.

Word spread quickly that the priest had touched the little girl with leprosy. By the time Father Damien arrived back in the colony with the load of lumber and the new band of lepers, the colony's citizens had gathered excitedly to see what was happening.

Father Damien announced that instead of using the lumber to build the church first, they would together build a hospital to care for the needs of the people. Isn't that what a church is supposed to be anyway—a hospital to care for the needs of the hurting, the wounded, and the broken?

In the story you see the transforming miracle of love. As Father Damien reached out and touched the untouchable, love came alive, and worked the miracle. Estranged, suffering, lonely people drew together in serving, caring, healing love for one another.

If there has ever been a time when we need for love to come alive in America, it is now.

There are many counterfeits of love because the human need for love is so great. If you are a woman reading these words and you cannot say that you ever heard your father say "I love you with all my heart", chances are great that you already have problems in relationships or marriage or that you will have. God is the source of love and if His love is not flowing through us then something is bottling it up. Godly parents need to love as God loves; redemptively, sacrificially and unconditionally.

Jealousy, often associated with love, as an example, is a self-centered attitude. How can you love someone so much that you want them for yourself only? You don't even want them looking at or talking to someone else. Jealousy is fearful of being displaced or replaced. It is an expression of fear and insecurity. It is possessive with an interest in self, not the other person. It is not love. Parents have been so possessive with their children that they crush the very life out of them.

Husband's have been so jealous and possessive that they want their wife at home at a certain time and always want to know where she is and what she is doing. That is not love. Love is trusting. Genuine love cannot flow through a heart that is primarily self-centered. Not only is this attitude destructive but just consider living with someone who wants to possess you. You cannot love this way. To be committed to live with someone that cannot love you and does not know how to express love but is damned up with feelings of resentment, jealousy, strife and conflict must be hell on earth. Love is not blind as some people say but rather it is super- sighted because you only know as much of another person as you unconditionally love.

People who have been brought up in situations where they have never observed love and do not know what kind of oneness can be expressed in genuine love must learn how to love and make a decision to love.

God's love is a winner in both life and death. God's love is the most positive force in the world. It is the destiny of man. No one can stop you from learning to love or making a decision to love but you. Remember, developing the right mental sets and attitude is crucial. Love is not a braggart. It does not encompass pride, egotism and arrogance. These negative mind sets are rooted in self and do not come from God. If you date someone that tells you how great they are, by the time the evening is over chances are you have had all of their greatness you can handle.

Sometimes there seems to be a way that is right but at the end of the path is death and destruction. Counterfeit love is such a path. Once in 1969, I was on patrol walking along a very narrow mountain path in the middle of the night above the Khe Sahn air strip in Vietnam. Suddenly, my platoon sergeant reached out and grabbed me, keeping me from plunging off a bluff to my death. The path seemed right to me. It was what I remembered. I was sure it would take me where I wanted to go but it was not real, it was counterfeit and at the end of that path was death. In a similar way, what we see today is the guilt and confusion associated with sex and the morally relaxed atmosphere that separates sex from commitment is such an example of love that is counterfeit. However, while the path was short that led to death that night in Vietnam, this path is often longer, spawning years later, a lack of intensity, trust, sexual dysfunction and relational emptiness. A healthy marriage has commitment at the heart of the relationship. And while many will rail against this position I would point out that the worm in the sour apple doesn't know its in one.

Intimacy is not sex, regardless of how we attempt to assimilate them. Intimacy is knowing and being known deeply. It is love. It requires time and effort. Sexual intimacies can occur without any of this happening. Love is emotional closeness that is vulnerable and trusting. Sex is an expression of love but it is not now nor ever has been its source. As I have mentioned before, like every other fundamental, love has at its base a spiritual foundation resting in a God that is the source. True love allows a person to surrender themselves completely to their partner and that sense of oneness is what makes the marriage relationship distinct among all other relationships. As I previously shared inner thoughts with you about my daughters, I am compelled here to pause and ask my darling and lovely wife to forgive me for the many years that I did not understand these truths. I was the worm in the sour apple. We want the warmth of true love and the thrill of real meaning it provides. We yearn for someone to care. We want someone whose love is strong enough to be free of manipulative self-interest. The truth is, this world knows very little about genuine love. How can someone love you or how can you love someone else if you put them down and elevate yourself? In fact, genuine love builds up, it does not tear down. Putting someone in a compromising position is not an expression of love. It might be lust but it is not love. Actually, the language of love and lust are the same. It is the heart or basic attitude that is different. One serves itself, the other serves others. Love always asks what is best for the other person. Genuine God-given love is the solution for every marriage problem, for every relational problem, for every problem period. Do you love people? Do the folks around you feel and sense your love? Are you someone who feels cheated out of love? Have you lived your life wondering what love is? God can answer all of these questions because it is His unlimited love flowing through us that empowers true love. One thing is certain, it would be the better part of discretion to be sure that a person knows how to love you before you marry them. It doesn't take a rocket scientist to spot someone that is hung up on themselves. You could be miserable for a very long time.

Love believes the best, expects the best, sees the best and stands ground in defense of the one loved. The one immutable truth of the fundamental of love is that it makes evident that life is like an echo shouting back at us with the attitude we offer: I LOVE YOU, I LOVE YOU, I LOVE YOU. Or, I HATE YOU, I HATE YOU, I HATE YOU. Surely, for the accurate thinker, there can be only one choice. The problem is like many of the other fundamentals of life we desire to master, we find it difficult to get the directions right or even hear them at times. A business associate of mine told me of an acquaintance who has a daughter that became deaf as a teenager. Her name was Kyle. He would often call home to his family and his wife would put Kyle on the phone to talk to him and while she was rambling away about her day he would keep repeating to her, "Kyle", I love you. – "Kyle", I love you. – "Kyle", I love you. Hoping that somehow his message would get through. That story always touches my heart because like Kyle we seldom hear God the Father as he continues to profess his love for us. We just keep rambling on about our day or our own problems or what we want, unable or unwilling to hear the message that God loves us. There is no force in the world as strong as a person who truly loves you.

Can you think of a life without love? There are people who cannot identify one single person in their life that genuinely loves them. Either that or like Kyle, they can't hear them. This is truly the height, width and depth of loneliness. How blessed are you if when you leave the house in the morning and someone says, "I love you and I will be thinking of you today." Suppose you lived in a palace and drove the best car and walked out of the door every morning with no one to say I'll be thinking of you or I love you. You just walk out alone. Love in it's false forms never solves these problems. You simply cannot give your life away to someone and at the same time try to squeeze everything out of them. Love reaches through, sees through, follows through, and is life's greatest power to influence. The message is clear, our longing for love and relationship are legitimate and God-inspired. What is required is a renewing of the mind and spirit so that we might walk down a path leading to life in all its fullness and not death. We are dependent creatures entering every relationship with self-interest and often manipulative self-protected unloving attitudes. We must be open to renewal. We must grope for a glimpse of the truth. God said He is Truth. God is Love. Love offers hope, hope that difficulties will pass, hope that the storm will soon be over, hope that the pain will soon be gone, hope that we will soon be over the mountain.

Finally, love allows us to be real. When our girls, Holly and Heather were small, I used to read them a story by Margery Williams entitled, *The Velveteen Rabbit*. In this story, the Velveteen Rabbit was asked the Skin Horse what it take to be real. "It doesn't happen all at once, said the Skin Horse. You become. It takes a long time. That's why it doesn't often happen to people who break easily, or have sharp eyes, or who have to be carefully kept. Generally, by the time you are real, most of your hair has fallen off and your eyes drop out and you get loose in the joints and very shabby. But these things don't matter at all, because once you are real you can't be ugly, except to people who don't understand."[26] Ultimately, loving is becoming real. Life is real, pain is real, hope is real, faith is real and yes, love is real. **Focus on love.**

RECOMMENDED READING:

Love Is A Decision: Smalley

Unconditional Love: John Powell

Love: Leo Buscaglia

America has never forgotten -
and will never forget -
the nobler things that brought her into being
and that light her path -
the path that was entered upon only
one hundred and fifty years ago ...

How young she is!

It will be centuries before she will
adopt that maturity of custom -
the clothing of the grave -
that some people believe she is already fitted for.

- Bernard M. Baruch

Pray that your loneliness may spur
you into finding something to live for,
great enough to die for.

- Dag Hammarskjîld

XI

FOCUS ON: DEATH AND TIME

Death casts its shadow over the land. As John Bright said to the House of Commons in 1855, "The Angel of Death has been abroad throughout the land, you may almost hear the beating of his wings." To die is a debt we all must pay. Death accepts no excuses. As Seneca pointed out, "A thousand approaches lie open to death."

Billy Graham referring to death as the Apocalypse had this to say: "The specter of the Apocalypse is found in abortion, abuse, addiction, brutality, crime, disease, drugs, hatred, lust, murder, neglect, pestilence, racial conflict, rape, revenge, starvation, suicide, violence and war. Fifty million deaths occur every year. Every year a million people die from man-made disasters. Eighty thousand die from earthquakes and ten thousand from floods.

Worldwide, there are 5 million malaria deaths per year and 3 million from tuberculosis; 1.8 million children die annually from vaccine preventable diseases, while infectious diseases kill 4 million unimmunized children. There are 5 million diarrhea deaths of children under the age of 5; and 4 million die of pneumonia. (There are potentially 60 million AIDS/HIV carriers with an infection growth rate of 100%). There are an estimated 3 million AIDS victims worldwide with a mortality rate of 100%.

Add to this an estimated 16.8 million who die from parasitic diseases, 1.3 million from circulatory disease, 5 million cardiovascular deaths, 4.3 million cancer deaths, 3.3 million perinatal deaths, 2.6 million tobacco-related deaths and 401,000 suicides every year.

In the United States, 50,000 people die in traffic accidents annually; 11,000 die from falls, 5,000 from fires and burns and 6,000 from drowning. Another 2,000 are killed each year by firearms; nearly 4,000 from ingestion and food objects; 1,000 are poisoned by gas; and 4,000 more die from other types of poison. There are 11 million alcoholics in this country and 76 million families have at least one member who is struggling with alcoholism or related problems.

How can anyone ever begin to comprehend the human toll of so much suffering, anguish, pain, and loss? Some 300 million people suffer from chronic or acute arthritis; there are 85 million severely handicapped children; and 900 million people who live in constant pain. There are 51 million certified psychotics and 10 million schizophrenics and 950 million psychoneurotics."[27]

As the weight of these statistics bear down on us, we must realize that our own end may be nearer than we anticipate. And in these days when Death rides the winds of the world, there is not a newspaper or television or radio report that does not make some reference to death. Fletcher and Beaumont in *The Woman Hater* had this to say of death, "This world's a city full of straying streets and death's the market place where each one meets." Henry Longfellow may have been contemplating all of this pain and anguish and sorrow when he wrote in Evangeline, "As she looked around, she saw how Death, the consoler, laying his hand upon many a heart, had healed it up forever."

"There are people," says Paul Tournier, "who go on indefinitely preparing for life instead of living it." You and I cannot afford to do that. As I learned in the killing fields of Vietnam, life is tissue paper thin. Death and time, Time and Death. Inextricably interwoven in a macabre dance. One concept constantly being wrestled with...time. The other concept constantly being ignored...death.

We live in a death-denying society. I previously addressed this issue in a conversation between Alexander Scott, "the preacher" and Corporal Dragin in book two of *The Memorial,* Dialogues of the Dead, Crown Books, 1989. Several young marines from Alpha Company were discussing life's purpose and exactly what they were all doing at that moment in Vietnam. Corporal Dragin, the cynic, had just commented that whether there was a purpose to life or not or whether life was worthless or not he just wanted to be given tomorrow and that perhaps, at best, life's purpose is no better than being able to still function sexually. Lieutenant Scott, (the preacher) was about to respond ...

"It was hotter. Rivulets of sweat ran down Alex's chest and mingled with the dried dirt that had taken up a position there for several days now. Several more troops had joined Sugar Bear and Boston. The Preacher was now attempting to respond to Dragin's question, and, turning to those left, he said, Solomon said that all is vanity. We are born, we live, suffer, die, then others come and do the same. They get up, go to work at the same place, doing the same work until they aren't needed anymore and are told they will never be forgotten; but they will be and they know it. They work, sleep, enjoy themselves, eat, make love, and it all starts over again. Nothing is ever really new and man can't seem to get outside the restraints of his own nature. Dragin is doing the same thing. He is just seeking life, he even said it. That's what all of us are doing, only we are in an environment where we can't ignore death.'

What do you mean by ignore death?' Sugar Bear asked. Bo Lawler had shuffled up by this time and was listening while he sipped on a warm Carling's Black Label. Alex, noticing him, lifted an eyebrow in recognition and continued.

"Think about it, Bear, we can't ignore death because it is so much a part of us every day. We see it, anticipate it, expect it, and yet, for the most part, even here, feel it will happen to someone else and not us. In the States, on the other hand, people not only feel it will happen to someone else but that it will never happen to them. Here, we know it will happen. That's why Corporal Dragin says, 'just give me tomorrow.' We all feel the same way but we are learning in the middle of this adventure how to face death because we cannot ignore it. That is why I am always on you guys to accept the Lord. Everybody comes face to face with Him someday. You must be prepared for this because it will not only be the single greatest adventure you will ever have but will be the only one that will never die."

And while we are on the topic of war, war does not increase death because death is complete in every generation. It might be interesting to note the epidemiology of death in war over the last four centuries:

17th century - average annual rate of death was 9500

18th century - 15,000

19th century - 13,000

20th century - 458,000 per year ... so far

Interestingly, there was just an average of 6000 military deaths per year during the Thirty Years War of the first half of the 17th century for a total of about 180,000 killed. By comparison, more than 250,000 died during just four years of the American Civil War some 250 years later. But more shocking, is that 5,561,000 combat deaths per year occurred during WW II, for a total of more than 30 million soldiers killed, not including the more than 20 million civilian deaths.

Yet, with all of this, we still live in a death denying society.

While the irreversible fact is, that no matter what your diet, no matter how much you exercise or how well you eat, no matter how low your cholesterol level happens to be, someday you will die. It is also interesting to me that we are focusing on the fundamentals of how to face life but it is, how we deal with death and tragedy that says so much about what kind of people we really are. Richard Selzer in *Down From Troy* reflected one attitude toward death when he wrote about a discussion he had with his father shortly before his death. "Why does everyone have to die?" I once asked him. "It's not fair."

"It is fair," he corrected. "It's part of being a person. It would be much worse not to." Another time he told me, "People are like old paintings. They can be temporarily restored, but there comes a time to die. Besides, people are braver than you think."[28]

What are some of the other observations people have had about death?

"Death and the sun are not to be looked on with a steady eye."

"Death devours lambs as well as sheep."

"Death keeps no calendar."

"Death meets us anywhere."

"Death pays all debts."

"Every door may be shut but death's door."

"There is a remedy for all things except stark death."

And what of time? We all live on borrowed time. Time is immensely valuable and utterly irretrievable. In fact, it is the most valuable commodity we have. Through time, we rush toward death.

What are some of the things that people have to say about time?

"Time goes by."

"Time is money."

"Spend time wisely."

"Time flies."

"Time will take care of it."

"I don't have time."

"The tyranny of time."

"Save time."

"Time will tell."

Truly, time has some very strange qualities. It goes much faster for the dentist than the patient. It is slower for the student than the teacher and the congregation than for the preacher. It has supersonic capabilities in times of happiness and seems without end in times of tragedy. To the youth time is theoretical. To the old it is a fact. While we attribute many life-like qualities to time, it is but a measurement, a dimension. Our supply is totally perishable. It would seem that a clear understanding of time would give us a sense of urgency in life. It is the raw material from which life is made. Time does not go by, we do. In fact, it is not time that we have to manage but ourselves. There are volumes written on time management and how to effectively save time when the truth is, we can't save time at all. We can only apply personal discipline to managing ourselves.

It is clear that one of the reasons it is so important to understand the meaning and purpose of life, as well as establishing values and priorities, is that only then can we live life with a real sense of privilege and responsibility. This, then, manifests itself in the way we use our time. Our personal lives are molded into the image of our priorities. There always seems to be enough time to do what we should do if we have priorities established. God never requires of us movement in a direction for which we have not been allocated the appropriate time. Consequently, in relation to time, all roads ultimately lead back to management of ourselves. Indecision, vacillation, procrastination all die at the hands of self-discipline. This is what sets people apart. In the United States Marine Corps Drill Instructor School, there is a creed that states, "Self-discipline is that which next to virtue, truly and essentially raises one man above another." So, while no one has more or less time than anyone else and while we cannot really save time, we can, by self-discipline, do things more effectively or eliminate things we should not do at all.

Time is the currency we exchange for life. It takes us to and through good times, bad times, happiness, joy, troubles, temptations, ultimately, death. We each get 1440 minutes a day and 168 hours a week. It seems that while no one has enough time, everyone has all the time there is. During time, nations rise and fall. Generation after generation disappear. More than forty million people die every year and every four years more people die in the world than make up the entire population of the United States. If you live to be eighty years old, four billion people have died while you have lived. The statistics on death, as George Bernard Shaw once wrote, are very impressive. One out of one people die. Time and death are absolutely interlocked. In *Psalm 39:9*, it is written that if we want to make the most of life, we need to face the fact that it is going to end. I've often heard sales people say that no one can say a meaningful yes until they have had the opportunity to say no. In the mix of life and death and time, only those that are prepared to die are really prepared to live.

Every day of our lives, we are but a breath away from eternity. Different people respond different ways. Some defy death. Others are fatalistic and reject it. Others live in constant paralytic fear of death. Like time there is a mystery to death. It does not respect the young or the old, the good or the bad, the God-fearing or the pagan and, like everything else, it has been secularized in our society. The media has essentially given death over to an everything will be OK attitude and seldom approaches the subject unless in humor. But death is not humorous, it is final for this world. And like time, it does not heal. It is what we choose to do with both time and death that heals.

As Billy Graham says in his book *Facing Death* "The Hindu and the Buddhist view death as a means of being reincarnated. For many

Shiite Muslims killing the enemy or the infidel, especially the Christian or Jew, bring incomparable sexual pleasure in paradise this mind set drives behavior. It is increasingly clear that the way we view death and time determines the way we live our lives. We teach the facts of life but never the facts of death. Denying death comes from a disbelief in our own mortality. Life is sacred. The Germans killed 275,000 people before WWII practicing a euthanasia that was simply a bad attitude about life."[29] Both Helen Keller and Stephen Hawking would tell you there is no such thing as a life not worthy to be lived. Human life is a gift from God and is precious. In today's America, little by little, the sanctity of life is being eroded. We must hold sacred the human life. An ancient Arabian story illustrates this point. A servant once used a flute to beat rugs in his master's absence. He thought he was doing a good job but the master knew the flute was for making beautiful music, not beating the dust off rugs, and he raged against its misuse. Only when you appreciate the high value of something will you deplore its misuse. God knows what we were created for and deplores our misuse. The Bible tells us exactly what death is. Physical death is a separation of the spirit and soul from the body. But a far worse death is a spiritual death which is separation from God. The Scripture says, "the days of our lives are three score and then, and if by reason of strength they be fourscore yet is their strength and labor and sorrow, for its place soon be cut off and we will fly away." With all of the medical skill we have accumulated, the average life span is still seventy years. In *James 4:14* it is written, "So what is your life? Even a vapor that appeareth for a little while and then vanisheth away." Am I ready? How then shall I live? "Seeing all these things shall come to pass, what manner of person ought ye to be?" (*2 Pet. 3:11*)

Billy Graham and Grady Weln were ministering in Korea during the war. It was Christmas Eve and the Marines they were with had just lost a skirmish. Margaret Higgins who would later win the Pulitzer Prize for her work was interviewing this grizzled combat Marine Sergeant. It was forty below zero and he was tired and dirty and worn. He sat before her as one of the scarecrows of war. Ice had formed on his beard. Margaret, studying his face, asked him if he could have anything he wanted and she had the power to command it at that very moment what would he want. She expected him to say that he wanted a bath, or maybe a big steak, hot and piping, with a baked potato dripping with butter and sour cream. Or maybe even his wife or girlfriend or a loved one would be the answer. But as she looked in that haggard and hollow face he said the same thing that Corporal Dragin said in *The Memorial*..."Just give me tomorrow." Time is what we want. A new beginning. An opportunity for another chance. Whether in love, forgiveness, relationship or life, God is a God of new beginnings. It is only the legalistic moralists of our day that seem to take great joy in burying the wounded from life's battles. God knew the value of time far more than we could ever comprehend. For with each second comes another chance. The good news is God is a God of new beginnings. And He has an eternity to make it right.

There is no such thing as being a success in life without being conscious of time. We do not control time, it is something to which we adjust ourselves. Sometimes we want to stop it and other times we want to speed it up. Time, like life, is God-given. God set it in motion. Our life is an existence in a segment of this thing called time. It does not move faster, but at the same rate every day. It is we who fill our minds and hearts with things that make it feel as if time were flying or as if it were stuck. It is time that puts a period at the end of each second. It is time that will not allow us to retract words or actions misspent. It is the one thing that God gives us that no one else can alter. It is important to remember our past and think about how we have invested or spent our time and how we have invested or spent our life. What is it that we are putting off that is important to us? Our time, talent, intellect, will, mind, emotions, all of our gifts should be held sacred. If God has invested the gift of life and time in us, what kind of stewards are we with the gifts we have been given?

Are you thrilled with what you are doing? If you could change your schedule, how would you change it? Is there something in your attitude you would change? If your heart and priorities are right, then you will invest your time wisely. Time is also the essence of the life of love. It is impossible to have a happy marriage without the investment of time. Home, children, relationships, vocation all require time. What decision do you need to make next in your life?

In Kahima, Nagaland there is a plaque that marks the place where the Japanese advance was halted in India during WWII. The inscription on the plaque reads, "We gave today so that you may have a tomorrow." God gave his son so that you and I could have tomorrow. Our tomorrow is forever. Tomorrow belongs to the believer. Yes, God is a God of new beginnings. Death and time hold within their grasp only the admonition to keep sacred what has been freely given, life, in all its beauty and abundance. Life in all its pain and tragedy.

Happiness is a choice and grief is a certainty but life and time are gifts to be held both sacred and honored until we meet the final universal enemy. Death, the last enemy to be vanquished.

You and I take out life insurance because we know we are going to die. We will some day have to give an account of how we invested or spent this time. Without focus on fundamentals, we are at sea in this continuum of time waiting to perish. It is only moral courage that can make us indestructible. As with all of life's fundamentals there is a momentum to living by principles. Each act of courage adds to your faith in yourself, to your purpose and to dignity of life. Each brave act enlarges your ability to be brave until eventually the process is irreversible. Yet, as Ed Coles says, "no one can see anything with the lights out and God is the Light." Should we keep living the way we are living or should we change the direction of our life? God help us to live now in the light of a real tomorrow. **Focus on death and time.**

RECOMMENDED READING:

Storm Warnings: Billy Graham

Tyranny of Urgent: Charles Hummel

Denial of Death: Ernest Becker

One Minute Manager: K. Blanchard

The family - that great conservator of
national virtue and strength -
how can you hope to build it up in the midst of
violence, debauchery and excess?

- Mrs. Elizabeth Cady Stanton

The family is still the cornerstone of human development
no matter how complicated society may have become.

- Flemmie Kittrell

XII

FOCUS ON: FAMILY

I debated for some time about whether to include this fundamental in the manner I knew it should be written. At the end of the day, I knew I could make no choice but to speak the truth as I believed it to be. As a business leader, I am committed to renewing values. Public interest in business ethics ebbs and flows but seems to be at an all time high today. A general decline in ethical behavior begins long before people go to work. Family, church, school and friends have all contributed to shape moral character. In addition, today we have television, day care, and TV dinners that have stolen the platform from moral discourse. The declining secularization of society and the divergence of the conservative church have permitted birth control, abortion, alternatives to traditional marriage and a general distrust of the religious right to permeate society. All of this has led to the general breakdown of the nuclear family in America. Along with it, as Edmund Burke said, "An event is happening about which it is difficult to speak but about which it is impossible to remain silent."

Today, for many, what is legal is permissible and therefore what is legal is also moral. But as America stands at the crossroads we face a time of crisis and a time crying for national clarification of values. It is interesting that with so much danger in our society, statistically speaking, the most dangerous place for anyone to be, with regard to the preservation of life, is in the womb of a mother.

It seems that with a new definition of family and a utilitarian way of looking at life, that there are now lives not worthy to be lived. In fact, there are deaths that are deemed beneficial by virtue of relieving economic and financial burdens. No matter how hard it is to believe that someone would balance a life against money and conscience, we are seeing this today in America.

Are we really this philosophy? We have discussed a number of fundamentals. Each one has pointed us toward the capacity for living a better life and therefore contributing to a better America. But living a good life always exacts a price.

Today, children are taught that there are no values and higher education, particularly in moral philosophy and the humanities have not only denied traditional religious values but avoided moral indoctrination altogether. As James T. Engell of Harvard points out, there is no conscious guidance to ethical interpretation but rather technical, aesthetic and historical analysis of literature. The idea is to be noncoercive and intellectual rather than a moral role model.

Unfortunately, with this position comes no right or wrong and a denial of God. Hooked on our own pleasure we refuse to accept the challenge of love. We even alter nomenclature to rationalize bad ideas and bad thinking. Lying can be cast away as a "white lie." Adultery becomes "fooling around" and a baby that is to be aborted becomes a "fetus." It is interesting to note that you never hear an expectant mother saying, "I felt my fetus kick today." A baby only becomes a fetus if it is as the courts have classified, a non-person. As Dr. Bernard Nathan once queried, "If the abdominal wall of the pregnant woman were transparent, what kind of abortion laws might we have?"

Unfortunately, words or pragmatism or utilitarianism do not obviate sin. Our language and our country have been polluted through a denial of traditional values. This is not a question of choice as some would have us believe but it is a question of right and wrong. This is not a question of conscience as our conscience only appeals to the highest ideals we happen to embrace. And that is different for many people. When we focused on the fundamental of Choice, we learned that choosing to take a path is a destiny that will not be denied. That when we embraced one choice, we also choose to give up something else. We are at the crossroads America. We are the casualty of our own choices. Our lives and our country are being shaped by those that choose to love us and by those that do not.

Abortion is killing! It is sin. It is a choice and it is a true reflection of who we have become. I ask you this day, do you choose to love? Does love discriminate? Does love demand perfection? Does love rest on convenience and finance? Does love view people as expendable, disposable, and exploitable or as unique, special and worthwhile?

In the mad dash to escape from freedom and the absolutes that make up our Judeo-Christian heritage, we scoff at morality and ethics and biblical absolutes and become paranoid and schizophrenic in our attempt to deal with life. We spend time, energy and money to save the spotted owl, the snail darter and the whale. We perform surgery in the womb of a woman to save one baby and abort 1.5 million others yearly. We prohibit young people from buying booze and cigarettes and then give them condoms without telling their parents.

Having spent time in combat as a United States Marine, making life and death decisions, I feel qualified to say that life is a gift. Having looked down the barrel of a rifle and seen a human being in the cross hairs of a sniper scope, I feel qualified to ask the question, when is it right to take a life? Many of the same people who stand outside penitentiaries protesting pending executions favor abortion. If we can't kill babies after birth when is it OK? How about just before leaving the birth canal? How about one minute before or one hour or one day? How about one month? When is it right to kill this baby? Perhaps we should simply wait three days after birth as Dr. James Watson recommends and then all parents could have the same choice and save a lot of misery and suffering.

What is right and wrong is not a legal or majority view issue. We cannot embrace the idea that there is a life unworthy to be lived. That is the very premise that Hitler began with. It is the same premise that Dr. Jack Kevorkian embraces today as he goes about mirroring this slide in our national morality. Too often these people do not understand the result of their own teaching. They don't know where they are going or where they will end up. Often with good hearts and pure motives they simply see issues they want altered or conditions they would like to change. However, many times in later years, they would like to go back and retrace these steps but it is too late. I remember the great injustice Jane Fonda perpetrated on many young men during the Vietnam War. Encouraging these young soldiers and marines to disobey while she herself physically embraced the enemy, she left a wake of destruction in her path. Ms. Fonda then got on a plane and flew home while these young men had to live with the legacy she left behind. Today, while she may repent of those actions, others still suffer, while she came home to prosper off of the very system she earlier deplored. Again, often people don't face the conclusion of their own teaching.

Fifty years ago, Friedrich A. Hayek made that same point in his book *The Road to Serfdom*. Totalitarianism seemed to be the wave of the future in the 1930's. Fascism, Communism and Nazism seemed to foreshadow new forms of collectivism all over the world. While received well in Europe, the intellectual climate in America found publishers refusing to print Hayek's work which attacked all form of collectivism. It seems that socialism, while strong as an ideal, couldn't withstand the mess of reality for the Europeans that actually lived under it. Just like Jane Fonda in her day, unable to see beyond the war in Vietnam to the consequences of her teaching years later. We see the same thing continuing today where "only in America" are there substantial numbers of adherents to Marxism as a creed for its own sake. As Thomas Sowell pointed out in the January 17, 1994 issue of *Forbes*, "At the heart of the socialist vision is the notion that a compassionate society can create more humane living conditions for all through government "planning" and control of the economy. Both the moral and the efficiency arguments for socialism depend crucially on what Hayek called "intellectual *hubris*" - the assumption that we have such comprehensive knowledge that the only things lacking are such subjective factors as compassion and will.

Socialists are "dangerous idealists," according to Hayek, including many people "whose sincerity and disinterestedness are above suspicion" and individuals "of considerable intellectual distinction." The denigration and demonizing of political opponents, which has been an integral part of the vision of the left for at least two centuries was no part of Hayek's vision. Socialists to him were people who overestimated what was possible and underestimated the dangers created in pursuit of their ideals.

Socialists have "prepared the way for totalitarianism," according to Hayek, though they are themselves morally incapable of doing the hideous things necessary to make a totalitarian state work, and will draw back before following the inescapable logic of their vision to its conclusion - leaving the field to those whose ruthlessness is equal to the task. It is interesting to note, in some sort of ironic twist of history today, we see the birth of democracy in Mainland China spurred only by these writings of Hayek that were previously banned.

This politicizing of all sorts of non-political activities is flourishing today among the political left in all sorts of American institutions, including especially educational institutions where "politically correct" views are the clear goal of those for whom education is seen as the continuation of politics by other means.

The real issue, as Sowell points out, is not what anyone intends but what consequences are in fact likely to follow. I make the point again. Too often people simply do not understand the result of their own teaching and do not stick around long enough to bear the consequences. Hayek called them "the totalitarians in our midst." Sowell adds to this list of "modern day examples such as advocates of affirmative action, environmental extremists, AIDS activists, radical feminists, and all others who want their agendas carried out "at all costs." None advocates totalitarianism though all are moving the society in that direction, because only more centralized government power can deliver what they want."[30]

The rule of law, which Hayek saw as crucial, both to the economy and to the survival of freedom, is nowhere in greater danger than in the Supreme Court of the United States. With two or three exceptions, the Justices seem determined to be philosopher-kings, deciding issues according to "evolving standards" rather than fixed principles, and responsive to self-styled "thinking people" rather than to the written Constitution or the statutes passed to express the will of the voting public.

In the Supreme Court and elsewhere, blithe talk about "a living Constitution" conceals the fact that the Constitution is in fact dying as it is being reinterpreted out of existence, whenever it stands in the way of the prevailing *zeitgeist*."

While it may not be the prevailing zeitgeist of today, I submit organizations today must be run with the principle that people are first and objectives second. This is true in life. This is also right because people are the most valuable asset a company has. People have value. They are unique. Every working person knows this is true in their own heart and will work ceaselessly for an organization that believes this principle. Yet some of these same people who desperately want to be seen as valuable do not recognize this truth for the pre-born or the very old. You cannot have it both ways. We are at the crossroads because we have been stupid and wrong. We have traded in God's best for broken homes, divorce, incest, abused wives and children, abortion and rampant homosexuality. Listen to me. We are only as good as our deepest principles and our values. People long for hope but refuse to embrace truth because it requires faith. So instead, because it is easier to believe, we listen to the counsel of despair while meaning, hope, love, forgiveness and charity all die. The challenge to overcome this is not just cultural, it is spiritual. There are forces in America at work that are anti-family.

What happens to the moral fabric of a nation when 60% of marriages fail, when abortion is on demand and radical special interest groups dominate? This is what is confronting you and I at the crossroads today. It is a question of attitude, values and the worth of life. Our self esteem as individuals or as a nation is related to what we value most. We become virtually indistinguishable from the things we idolize. What we focus on is where we end up and that may be on the same trash heap where we discarded everything else we professed to love.

Money, cars, homes, clothes, hot tubs, furs and diamonds have enslaved us not freed us. Proud, arrogant, loving things and using people we have forgotten the values we once stressed. We are lost and not sure how to get back. Life is wasted in the endless pursuit of that which brings nothing. As Solzhenitsin said, "We always pay dearly for chasing after what is cheap!" Ego-centered, shallow and superficial we counterfeit truth and embrace a morality of economics unable to see our true reflection in the mirror.

As we stand at the crossroads today, before we choose the path we are to take, let's ask ourselves a few questions. What is it that we value most? What is our dominant thought on a daily basis? Where is our greatest pleasure? What is our dream? What values do the answers to these questions reflect? Do faith, morality, integrity, honesty, trust, respect and accountability have any role here? What about caring and giving? What is the attitude of our heart?

Do we subsidize the lazy and the self-indulgent? Do we create a breeding ground for poverty by feeding the lazy? Are we destroying the family? Have we confused loving our children with giving them things? It is in the family where we learn what life is all about. It is the family where character and habits and destiny are sown. We must leave our children a heritage that reflects those values that are worth duplicating. This is a spiritual issue. Only man could be so arrogant as to deny God His very existence and in the process remove all need for values of any kind. We are reaping what we have sown and we must choose a different path. We must recreate moral values in the family. It is the family that is the bedrock of society. We must reinvent, renew and reenergize the family and our country by focusing on love and encouragement.

As Jack Kemp said, government can only succeed when founded on the family. If the family collapses, our future will suffer irreparable damage. America is in turmoil and the family is in turmoil. As tragic as the earthquake in Los Angeles, the moral earthquake that is shattering values and collapsing homes is cracking the foundation of America. The family is under attack from everywhere. Because there are no moral absolutes or values that act as bedrock, our society swings back and forth with each new temblor.

Our children must once again find a place where solid values and relationships can be developed. The generation of 76 million Americans I grew up with called "baby boomers" have largely discarded the concepts that provided purpose and direction for their lives. Having grown up in what might have been the most pernicious environment in American history, we have made damaging choices that have removed the family as a God-ordained institution founded on a one woman and man relationship. Some of us are reconsidering these choices and their results and suggesting that perhaps the family of the future needs to be renewed by focusing on the basics of the past and returning to the heritage of our forefathers. We will either preserve or destroy our culture in the family. Within that environment, basic values such as chastity prior to marriage, self-discipline, work ethic, fidelity, loyalty and faith must be nurtured. It is here where our children will learn how to live in society. It is within the framework of the family that the future of America will be written. The family is the anchor for the ship of state where self-esteem and decent values will either be embraced or trampled upon, replaced by pragmatism, utilitarianism and nihilism. We must reject the egoism of Thomas Hobbes that postulates people act only in their self interest and the existentialism of Jean-Paul Sartre that says the final arbiter of right or wrong is the free will of the decision maker. It is this thinking that has left the moral person in life or business too often on their own. There is a large gulf between formal philosophy and the mess of reality. As I have said before, there is a unified body of knowledge available that has a beginning, a middle and an end. It supersedes Jeremy Benthem, John Stuart Mills, Immanuel Kant and others, offering moral based values for direction and forgiveness in the face of failure. God does have the answer and He has written it down. But simply moving God around like some giant chess piece is not the answer either. As David McCartney wrote, "I taught school for nearly 40 years and was never aware that God or prayer had been taken out of public schools. I was aware, however, that fewer and fewer students came to school knowing the Lord's Prayer, or having ever heard their parents pray or say grace at breakfast or dinner. Or even having breakfast. During my years in the American public schools system, I noted that more and more students had learned from home more about preying than about praying.

Some seem to think our God is something that we can move, remove, take out, put back - in our schools, our homes and our political institutions. What an odd concept of an all-powerful, all-knowing, ever-present God that is! The creator of the universe, this great God almighty, can be circled, hitched, tied up and untied, taken out, put back, packaged, unpackaged and sent packing, by a town, a school board, a commissioners court, a politician, a political party. And prayer is something we can take out like a seam in a too tight garment because of weight gain, and can be put back when we lose that weight...

We need a new church. The Church for the Emancipation of God From the Arrogance and Stupidities of Mankind. Maybe it could put God back in our pulpits, our pews, our homes, in our commissioner's courts and legislatures, and at our breakfast and dinner tables. Perhaps then, when children go to public school, they will have come from families where there is no racial hate, no live-in lovers, no liars or thieves, no lazy bums, no drug and alcohol misusers, no wife-, husband- or child-abusers and no tax or Medicare cheaters.

Perhaps, then, children will come to school clean in body and mind. They will have had a hot prayer-blessed breakfast with a momma and daddy at the table with them, and their homework will have been done. Momma and daddy will have shown enough interest for their child's education to have done what they should have been doing all these years they were living selfishly and ignoring the children they begat."[31]

C. S. Lewis pointed out in *The Abolition of Man* when we abandon the transmission of values, we end with social fragmentation and risk the very obliteration of humanity." What are these values? Perhaps our forefathers were right. Perhaps God is right. The values we need that can shape the family and America can be found in His word. It is not even necessary to believe in Him to receive the benefit. How can anyone argue with values that were exhibited in the life of Christ? Is not love, compassion, giving, fidelity, loyalty, honesty, trust and mercy of greater worth than the hate, greed, pride, anger, envy and lust that is destroying the American family? What is it that we are ripping from the womb of

America? Along with the loss of lives of these precious children comes a national legacy of guilt and shame. Addiction, disease, psychological turmoil, family conflict and death remain. What is left? People who no longer know where they stand. In the quest to embrace diversity, beliefs are obliterated and the bedrock that remains is just so much pluralistic oatmeal. Where is the anchor?

The consequences are tearing apart our families and crumbling the foundation of our country. There is hope for the family and there is hope for America but it is grounded in traditional values that enable us to anchor in the right message. We need a sentinel in the watchtower. We need accountability. We all fail morally, spiritually, relationally and financially because we cannot see our own weaknesses. Families, business, jobs, savings and relationships are being lost because of compromise, deceit and wrong thinking. Let's reconnect ourselves to love and unselfish giving. Let's take back our country and renew its heart, one child at a time, one person at a time, one family at a time. **Focus on family.**

RECOMMENDED READING:

Maximized Manhood: Cole

Spirit Controlled Family Living: LaHaye

After Every Wedding Comes A Marriage: Florence Littauer

Four Pillars of A Man's Heart: Stu Weber

*If we believe there is no hope for man
and no future for civilization,
then morality is a meaningless illusion;
life "is a tale" told by a divine idiot,
"full of sound and fury, signifying nothing,"
and our existence is an obscene and
impious joke, jocularly and malevolently
formulated by a supreme Demon for the
malicious purpose of humiliating and degrading man.*

- William B. Silverman

*A Nation which does not remember
what it was yesterday, does not
know what it is today, nor what it is
trying to do. We are trying to do a futile
thing if we do not know where we come from
or what we have been about.*

-Woodrow Wilson

XIII

FOCUS ON: HEROES & HOPE

Within the pages of the unified body of knowledge I have been referencing, The Bible, can be found the keys to the success and failure of America and the world. America has survived and prospered because men of faith wrote into our founding documents the truth about God. In fact, The Declaration of Independence calls God the Source of Rights, the Creator and the Supreme Judge of the World. The Bible itself points out that man without the Bible is a law unto himself, accusing or excusing. Jesus said, "if you abide in my Word...you shall know the truth and the truth shall set you free."

Instead, we find America fleeing from freedom without God and without love. To the Puritans that founded our country, growing up uneducated meant moral debasement and religious error.

They knew that people who were instructed in principles from the Bible and great literature were better citizens. They also knew this firm foundation in principled education was a powerful weapon against tyranny and political and social irresponsibility. Walter Williams reflected on this recently when he wrote, "Our fiscal problems stem from a long, relentless retreat from the moral principles established by our Constitution.

Social or entitlement spending accounts for the bulk of runaway spending and the resulting deficits and debts over the last several decades. Crop, welfare and business handouts are little more than congressionally imposed obligations on one set of citizens for the benefit of another.

The church, legal scholars, the occasional politician and a sense of do-right by citizens at large used to be our moral anchor. These people, values and institutions, that once served us well, are today either ignorant or contemptuous of our Constitution. Without a moral anchor, we're adrift in a sea of immorality, headed toward economic and social chaos.

Our law schools are little more than dens of iniquity that nurture and breed the constitutional derelicts we have in Congress, before the bar and on the bench. Ask a lawyer what's the constitutional authority for government's imposing obligations on some to provide what has become known as entitlements for others. You'll get grossly ignorant answers, ranging from it's in the constitution to promote the general welfare to it's the government's responsibility. If that lawyer graduated from one of our more prestigious schools, he'll lecture you that the Constitution was written when times were simpler. It's a "living document" adaptable to the complexities of today.

Balderdash! A constitution establishes "rules of the game," standards of conduct amongst people and their government. For game rules to have meaning and usefulness and be just, they can't be "living." How would you like to play poker with me? There you sit with three of a kind, and I tell you my pair of aces wins because Hoyle's rules, our poker constitution, have been adapted to the complexities of my life.

Established churches are equally contemptuous of constitutional and moral principles. Ministers and bishops differ little from other Washington hustlers who beg and promise constituent votes as a means to persuade congressmen to use the power of their office to confiscate that which rightfully belongs to one American and give it to those the ministers think should have it.

While your bishop or minister may support government welfare, food stamp or housing programs, ask him whether he supports the methods whereby government obtains the resources. More specifically, ask him whether he can show the Christian basis for using force to take what belongs to one person to give it to another. If it's OK in his book for government to do it, ask him what does he think of it being done privately. The latter is called theft.

Although your minister won't come out and say it, he probably believes that the commandment "Thou shalt not steal" applies only to private acts. But if there's a majority vote, and it's done by government, it's no longer theft in the eyes of God, but charity. How morally shallow can one be?

Widespread retreat from morality is the bad news. The good news is Americans have never done wrong things for a long time. We need to come to our senses and try to set things right. I hope I live to see it."[132]

Somehow we have reached the point where we are taught upside down and backwards. The entitlement clause of the first Amendment having been enlarged and the free exercise clause having been diminished, we are unable to tap into America's history and culture and are now vulnerable to tyranny. We have learned no lessons from the past. We live in a country that has professed to be "One Nation Under God." Yet, we have taken God out of our schools and must pretend that He no longer exists. In fact, we now exist in a politically correct environment where Christianity is considered a haven for right wing religious zealots and is now a threat to our nation.

Charles Darwin believed nothing from the past had value because it was outdated. He felt the past, with it's religious and cultural heritage, was inferior. But what has happened since we removed God from the classroom? Our schools have produced an adult population that is 1/3 illiterate. Twenty-five million Americans can't read and while we have liberated our schools from prayer, we have also liberated the lusts of the flesh. It seems that we have educated our children about sex and in the process increased the birthrate some 200% from 1960-1980. But Darwin was wrong. We can learn from the past. What we can learn is what we stand for, not how much we can tolerate for the sake of embracing diversity. We don't need a new covenant today as some politicians state. We need to honor the one we already have. We have slammed the door in the face of God in Washington and in our homes all hell is breaking loose. We have erected our own idols, and proclaimed our own standards. The covenant in marriage is between three people, the husband, the wife and God. The covenant our country was founded upon and grew in was between the American people and God. Who is the new covenant with, that Mr. Clinton and others are referencing and why do we need it? The problem is not political, it is spiritual. No action is morally neutral. Every decision has an economic and spiritual consequence and we are all accountable. Whether as individuals or as a country you and I cannot cover up sin by putting a condom on it.

Regardless of what the historical revisionists have to say, the United States of America was established as a nation ruled by law and these laws were to conform to God's law. This is what "unalienable" rights were all about. They were retained beyond society because they were God- given. The signers of the Declaration understood this. And this is precisely why our freedom has prevailed while so many others have fallen to tyranny. We have replaced God with ourselves and we will realize that without Him we are blind. We need to know where we are going again and this is why it is so important to remember. There were and there are real heroes and there is hope!

No matter what you are told by the sophisticated classes that see virtue in every form of corruption and corruption in every form of virtue, I think you know, as I do, that the American people hunger for acts of integrity and courage. The American people hunger for a statesman magnetized by the truth, unwilling to give up his good name, uninterested in calculation only for the sake of victory, unable to put his interests before those of the nation. What this means in practical terms is no focus groups, no polls, no triangulation, no evasion, no broken promises and no lies. These are the tools of the chameleon.

They are employed to cheat the American people of honest answers to direct questions. If the average politician, for fear that he may lose something, is incapable of even a genuine yes or no, how is he supposed to rise to the great occasions of state? How is he supposed to face a destructive and implacable enemy? How is he supposed to understand the rightful destiny of his country and lead it there?[33]

The morally bankrupt pens of today may have not only bludgeoned John Wayne and Roy Rogers and Sky King and Ozzie and Harriet into the rarefied atmosphere of ridicule, but they also take great delight in both destroying and sensationalizing every weakness any hero our heritage has ever had. Even Abraham Lincoln has not been able to escape these modern Pharisees.

Yet, America would not have come out of the Civil War as it did had it not been led by men like Lincoln and Lee. The battles raged for five years, but for 100 years the country, both North and South, modeled itself on their characters. They exemplified almost perfectly Churchill's statement that "public men charged with the conduct of the war should live in a continual stress of soul." Whereas a statesman knows continual stress of soul, a politician is happy, for he knows not what he does.

When letters took a month by sea and the records of the U.S. government could be moved in a single wagon pulled by two horses, we had great statesmanship. We had men of integrity and genius: Washington, Hamilton, Franklin, Jefferson, Adams, Madison, and Monroe. These were men who were in love with principle as if it were an art, which, in their practice, they made it. They studied empires that had fallen for the sake of doing what was right in a small country that had barely risen and were able to see things so clearly that they surpassed in greatness each and every one of the classical models that they had approached in awe.

Now, lost in the sins and complexity of a Xanadu, when we desperately need their high qualities of thought, their patience for deliberation, and their unerring sense of balance, we have only what we have.

Which is a political class that in the main has abandoned the essential qualities of statesmanship, with the excuse that these are inappropriate to our age. They are wrong. Not only do they fail to honor the principles of statesmanship, they fail to recognize them, having failed to learn them, having failed to have wanted to learn them.

In the main, they are in it for themselves. Were they not, they would have a higher rate of attrition, falling with the colors of what they believe rather than landing always on their feet-adroitly, but in dishonor. In light of their vows and responsibilities, this constitutes not merely a failure but a betrayal, and not only of statesmanship and principle but of country and kin.[34]

What is left in the wake of this destruction is a nation in anxiety. No longer able to trust God, knowing we are just as sinful and guilty and evil as everyone else, we are left breathless by disclosure after disclosure relating to those we have admired. If the point to be made is that these people are human, fine. But by denigrating the good as well as the bad, by focusing on the error and not that part that knew greatness and courage, and honor, is to leave the cynics behind closed doors sneering and laughing at those that pursued the dream when they never had the courage to try.

Here is the truth. We are all "weeble wobbles." We feel bad about feeling good. We feel guilty about feeling not guilty. I am honest but I still play games. I am an angel that can have an incredible capacity for beer. Why can't we be honest with each other about the capacity for greatness and sin that resides in each of us. We know what breaking the covenant of the past has left us. We have a crisis of confidence. We have a crisis of faith. It comes pouring forth in the news that surrounds the S & L crises and the Wall Street scandals. We are shocked at the BCCI rip off and the sex exploits of politicians. We can't believe check bouncing by congress or religious leaders caught with their pants down. And the rest of the world has not escaped. From Robert Maxwell in England to the Prime Minister of Japan, scandal and outrage permeate the world.

We feel betrayed. We are disappointed. We both want and need leadership. We want to know if there is any leader who has the strength of character to sustain faith and be truthful. The answer is that the process of leadership and nation building itself is amoral. Hitler, Stalin, Manson, Koresh and Saddam Hussein all had strong beliefs about conduct but they were evil. As Allan Bloom pointed out, no one seems to know the true nature of evil today. We cannot leave things in the hands of people who hold only a negative view of life. We must put God back where He belongs, we must put our heroes back where they belong and focus on the values and laws that speak life and not death. There is something cleansing and powerful and purging in doing what is right.

The heart of America must be transformed one person at a time and only God can transform hearts. We live in a culture that has gone morally berserk. As Darrell Bock recently said, "Our country has been on a 30-year experiment in which religion has been relegated to the parking lot in the game of public discourse. The issue is broader than school prayer. In its place have come videos, movies and TV shows filled with violence and blatant sexuality. People are treated as objects, not beings created equal in the image of God. This culture's food has been self-indulgence, raw anger and mind-blowing drugs.

What should we do? What about a playing field where public discourse is not left spiritually naked? I am not arguing for any particular religion here. I am just making a simple request to occasionally let God in the batter's box - and to let our children reflect on the concept that human life is precious because it is grounded in a greater level of being.

Even in Europe, public discourse allows religion a place. In Russia, where religion was severely repressed, a revival is going on, as its citizens recognize that there is more to life than greeting the rising sun each morning.

Here in America, it is as though we were trying to play basketball without hands or soccer without our feet. The most precious and deepest thoughts remain vaulted in the individual soul, rather than being put out on the table for discussion."[35]

In a similar vein, Bill Murchison, referencing Ann Landers and Hillary Clinton who were lamenting the state of America, adds this, "O brethren, O sistren, we're not talking here about Bible-walloping, mouth-foaming evangelists. We're talking about two modern secularists, wringing their hands as humanity plunges deeper into debasement.

I offer a friendly, low-stakes wager. It is that, for every politician or political groupie fretting over the federal deficit, 1,000 parents fret over our downward moral trajectory. Indeed, some of these would rejoin that the deficit - understood as a failure of thrift and foresight - is but one symbol of our moral plunge. We're going to hear more and more about that plunge this year, the next year, the rest of the decade and beyond. Get used to it.

One thing we'll hear is a laundry list of putative remedies to be sponsored by government, a fair number of these coming from Hillary Clinton herself. The question must then arise; What makes us think politicians would know a moral value if they saw it, far less know how to inculcate it? We may be headed toward a surge of concern not so much for moral values as for those religious truths on which all morality depends.

After all, a value is an opinion - take it or leave it. A truth *is*. It doesn't go away because you ignore it. That is essentially what modern society has been doing - in ignoring, in the interest of pluralism and good fellowship, the objective claims of religion. While an estimated 90 percent of Americans profess some kind of belief in some kind of God, a like percentage of the media elite say they never darken the door of a church. At that, they are typical of cultural and political leaders across the board, most of whom could more readily recite the baseball standings than the Apostles Creed.[36]

Michael Novak made similar observations in Forbes observing, "Film critic Michael Medved plays a game at Hollywood parties. He asks Hollywood types how many people they think go to church or synagogue every week in America. "No one I know," they often reply with a laugh.

"Seriously," Medved insists, "guess." Usually they guess about one percent; the highest estimate he has heard is ten percent. The correct answer, during any given week, is 40 percent.

Although the cultural elite may not realize it, most Americans already know what is sacred, and know it through religious traditions for which the year 2000 will not be the first millennium they have known."

There is something seriously wrong when it takes a federal judge to rule that the Boy Scouts of America may keep language about God in their oath. In a world full of violence and gangs, some thought of God may not be a bad idea. Perhaps, as we long for the kind of leadership and heroes that will define the future for America, we should consider the character of the man who is President and honorary head of the Boy Scouts as he snubbed the Scout Jamboree for the sake of his "new covenant." Apparently, the acid test for Bill Clinton's new covenant is pluralism.

"Actually it's the only test one hears about anymore. Tests of worth and efficiency, right and wrong, truth and falsehood, don't matter. It's nothing but look-how-inclusive-we're-becoming. Look how many outcasts' we're embracing. America as one giant therapeutic enterprise, designed not to maximize liberty and virtue but to make people Feel Good About Themselves - isn't that increasingly our national vision? If you call it vision.[137]

Feeling good about ourselves is not the American Dream. It is not the view that translates into morally fit children and morally fit adults. James Q. Wilson, a Professor of Management and Public Policy at the University of California at Los Angeles writing on character says that throwing more money into anonymous, principless, motivationless welfare programs is not the answer. What he talks about is culture and moral instruction. What he is saying makes the civil rights oriented liberal fringe jump right through the wall.

"I think what we face is the fact that our culture, as defined by the mass media and all to often by academic and political leaders, is a culture that still at its core emphasizes the rule: 'Do your own thing.' In recent decades...the collapse of the family and the collapse of community culture within inner-city areas has given a new urgency to the problem of youth crime."

What does he recommend that could (God forbid!) actually work? He suggests, first, moving children into an environment that is nurturing and that provides moral instruction. Since we "get more of what we subsidize," we should require teenagers on welfare to live with their parents; or in group shelters that provide a regular environment - and moral instruction or boarding schools that would serve as molders of morals for poor children.

In short, we know what the problem is: It is a lack of moral training and lack of socialization of children in our society. We know what the principle behind the problems should be - put these children in new constructs where they will have moral training.

His simple, wise ideas recall the late Joseph Campbell, the great anthropologist. After Mr. Campbell described a male puberty ritual in New Guinea that was admittedly brutal, journalist Bill Moyers asked him what happened to societies that did not have such socialization rituals. Mr. Campbell smiled wanly and said, "Just look around our big cities."

Mr. Campbell also delineated the important nature of the adult male's imprint on young males. "The father is more disciplinarian," he wrote. "He's associated much more with the social order and the social character. This is actually the way it works in societies. The mother gives birth to his nature, and the father gives birth to his social character."

Instead of discipline and respect for reasonable authority these last decades, we have had in its place the "self-esteem" movement. This is a fraud. Self-esteem comes not from phony assurances that you are wonderful when you are not. Self-esteem comes from early discipline that shows children their parents love them enough to create a secure and sensible world around them.[38] This is why we have created the Mail Boxes Etc. Foundation for Children's Initiatives along with the GOAD family with their inner city Jam Street initiatives at its core. It is our hope that we will be able to reach hundreds of thousands of children with values-based curriculum and life skills designed to bring a new generation of young people who remember their heritage and positively contribute to the future of America. In this way, we can transform the hearts of America one child at a time. If you would like further information about this foundation please write or call Mail Boxes Etc. Foundation for Children's Initiatives, 6060 Cornerstone Court West, San Diego, CA 92121, 619/455-8800.

Yes, we need to transform the heart of America. Yes, we need to understand the nature of the evil that is upon us. The heart of the human problem, is the problem of the human heart. We cannot be psychoanalyzed back to health. Education is not the answer. Environment is not the answer. Attitude is the answer and that is an inside job. Only God can transform the human heart. What American business is beginning to understand today is the same for American Government and the American people. There is no system or process that will fix the problem. It is people that run the systems and processes not systems that run the people. Only when a critical mass of people have taken accountability and responsibility for change will it take place. This requires transformational leadership. This deals directly with people and their attitudes and it can only happen one person at a time.

What we need is a restoration of our own identity. What we need are leaders and heroes. What we need is hope. We need men and women who have truly faced their mistakes and have known the forgiveness of God. When we lose contact with those things that remind us of where we came from and who we are we become a law unto ourselves.

"A nation which does not remember what it was yesterday, does not know what it is today, nor what it is trying to do. We are trying to do a futile thing if we do not know where we came from or what we have been about."[39]

On July 4, 1776, there was signed in Philadelphia one of America's historic documents. That document marked the birth of this nation which, under God, was destined for world leadership. The closing words of the Declaration of Independence were solemn: They were: "For the support of this declaration, with a firm reliance on the protection of the Divine Providence, we mutually pledge to each other, our lives, our fortunes, and our sacred honor." It is important to remember these things.

Fifty-six courageous men signed that document. Few of them would survive. Five would be captured by the British and tortured before they died. Twelve had their homes from Rhode Island to Charleston, sacked, looted, occupied by the enemy or burned. Two lost their sons in the Army. Nine of the 56 died in the war. None of them, however, lost their sacred honor. That has been preserved the world over by generations of Americans who have lived free. It is important to remember these things.

These men considered liberty much more important than the security they enjoyed. They pledged their lives, their fortunes, their honor - and they fulfilled their pledge. They paid the price. Freedom was won. It is important to remember these things.

Someone once said that to be born free is a privilege. To die free is an awesome responsibility, because freedom is never free. It is always purchased at great price. Where would we, who are citizens of the United States of America, be today if there had not been those who counted the cost of freedom and were willing to pay for it? Where will we be tomorrow if men and women of integrity do not come forward who are also willing to pay the price? It is important to remember these things.

John Quincy Adams said of us, "posterity - you will never know how much it has cost my generation to preserve your freedom. I hope you will make good use of it." It is important to remember these things.

And so it goes. God chose to bless America with abundance unprecedented in history and with freedoms that are the envy of the world. In my lifetime, half the world has gone to bed hungry and for most of my life half the world has lived behind the iron and bamboo curtain where freedom as we know it, did not exist. Still this magnet of freedom called America still draws more immigrants from other countries than any other nation on earth.

Through the decades, America has opened her heart to the poor of the world. She has given generously to every nation, even her enemies in times of emergencies. America, in fact, gives more to charitable, religious and philanthropic causes than any country on earth. America has also enacted more social legislation providing for more individual freedom than any other nation in the history of the world.

America did not just happen by chance. The great spiritual heritage that built America happened by a remarkable design, so did American democracy and our constitution and the great freedom that they assure. The path to glory has always been bathed in blood and tears. It is important to remember these things.

Listen America, we need renewal. We do not need a new covenant, we need to restore the one we already have. I am talking to you and me. This is not an issue of subsidies or government or process. It is a one-on-one spiritual issue of accountability and responsibility. You and I are a part of the fabric of life and what we do affects the profile of the whole. Our lives are not our own business. Restoring our identity personally and corporately brings us right back to responsibility. Today is the day to become the type of people we are dreaming of becoming. Today is the day to become the type of country we are dreaming of becoming. We have been caught between the sunlight and the shadows. It is time to remember our heroes and look up in hope, as Rabbi Abba Hillel Silver wrote:

Out of the bounty of the earth

and the labor of men;

out of the longing of the heart

and the prayers of souls;

out of the memory of ages

and the hopes of the world;

God fashioned a nation in love

and blessed it with a purpose sublime

and they called it America.

GOD BLESS AMERICA

Focus on heroes and hope.

James H. Amos, Jr.

RECOMMENDED READING:

The Light and the Glory: Peter Marshall

Great American Statesmen & Heroes: Millard

The Founding Fathers On Leadership: Phillips

NOTES

AUTHOR'S NOTE:

1   Helprin, Mark. Editorial Comment. <u>The Wall Street Journal</u> 2 July 1998.

2   Schroeder, Paula. "Viewpoints." <u>The Dallas Morning News</u> 14 March 1993.

PROLOGUE

3   Bradbury, Ray. "The Affluence of Despair." <u>The Wall Street Journal</u> 3 April 1998.

CHAPTER I: AT THE CROSSROADS

4   Cooke, Alistar. "Whither America." <u>Financial Times</u> 5 & 6 October 1991.

5   Slosser, Bob. <u>Changing The Way America Thinks</u>.

6   Bockmon, Marc and Randy Pennington. <u>On My Honor I Will</u>.

CHAPTER V: FOCUS ON: VALUES

7   Halprin, Mark. Editorial Comment. <u>The Wall Street Journal</u> 2 July 1998.

8   Neely, Greg. <u>The Dallas Morning News</u>, 2 February 1992.

9   Byrd, Sen. Robert. <u>Roll Call</u>.

10   Elsasser, Glen. <u>The Dallas Morning News</u>. 25 May 1992.

11   Lewis, Kathy. "Elections '92." <u>The Dallas Morning News</u> 18 May 1992.

12   Melvin, Ann. <u>The Dallas Morning News</u>. 5 June 1993.

13 Murchison, William. "Viewpoints." <u>The Dallas Morning News</u>. 19 February 1992.

14 Williams, Walter. <u>The Dallas Morning News</u>. 4 April 1992.

15 Leffel, Kristen. "The Value Store of Life." <u>America on My Mind</u>. Helena & Billings, Montana: Falcon Press, 1991

16 Williams, Walter. <u>The Dallas Morning News</u>. 29 August 1992.

CHAPTER VI: FOCUS ON: CHOICE

17 Cole, Edwin Louis. <u>On Becoming a Real Man</u>. Nashville: Thomas Nelson, 1992.

CHAPTER VII: FOCUS ON: LEADERSHIP

18 Thomas, Cal. "Viewpoints: Restoring the Good of Christmas." <u>The Dallas Morning News</u>. 23 December 1993.

19 Murchison, William. <u>The Dallas Morning News</u>.

20 Krug, Doug and Ed Oakley. <u>Enlightened Leadership</u>. Denver: Stone Tree Publishing, 1992.

CHAPTER VIII: FOCUS ON: RELATIONSHIP

21 Murchison, William. <u>The Dallas Morning News</u>. October 1991.

22 Murchison, William. <u>The Dallas Morning News</u>. 12 October 1991.

23 Editorial Comment. <u>Economist Magazine</u>. 12 August 1991.

CHAPTER IX: FOCUS ON: FORGIVENESS

24 <u>Essays, Speeches & Public Letter</u>. Random House.

25 Fairlie, Henry. <u>The New Republic</u>.

CHAPTER X: FOCUS ON: LOVE

26 Williams, Margery. <u>The Velveteen Rabbit</u>. New York: Doubleday & Co. Inc., 1930

CHAPTER XI: FOCUS ON: DEATH AND TIME

27 Graham, Billy. <u>Storm Warning</u>. Dallas: Word Publishers, 1992.

28 Selzer, Richard. <u>Down from Troy</u>. New York: William Morrow & Co., 1992.

29   Graham, Billy. <u>Facing Death</u>.

CHAPTER XII: FOCUS ON: FAMILY

30   Sowell, Thomas. "A Road to Hell Paved." <u>Forbes</u>.
     17 January 1994.

31   McCartney, David. "Viewpoints: Voting the Almighty Back In."
     <u>The Dallas Morning News</u>. 1993.

CHAPTER XIII: FOCUS ON: HEROES AND HOPE

32   Williams, Walter. <u>The Dallas Morning News</u>. 9 October 1993.

33   Helprin, Mark. <u>The Wall Street Journal</u>. 2 July 1998.

34   Helprin, Mark. <u>The Wall Street Journal</u>. 2 July 1998.

35   Bock, Darrell. <u>The Dallas Morning News</u>. 22 May 1993.

36   Murchison, William. <u>The Dallas Morning News</u>. 16 June 1993.

37   Murchison, William. <u>The Dallas Morning News</u>.
     18 November 1992.

38   Geyer, Georgie Anne. <u>The Dallas Morning News</u>.
     31 August 1993.

39   Woodrow Wilson.